HOW TO
BUY A HOME WHILE YOU CAN STILL AFFORD TO

MICHAEL C. MURPHY

REVISED EDITION

 Sterling Publishing Co., Inc. New York

Sample mortgage form reprinted courtesy of Chesterfield Federal Savings and Loan Association of Chicago.

Mortgage tables reprinted by permission of Bogdan Kaczmarek.

Library of Congress Cataloging-in-Publication Data
Murphy, Michael C. (Michael Charles), 1950–
  How to buy a home while you can still afford to.
  Includes index.
  1. House buying—United States. I. Title.
HD1379.M83 1986   643′.12   86-963
ISBN 0-8069-6312-3 (pbk.)

Revised edition
Copyright © 1986, 1981 by Sterling Publishing Co., Inc.
Two Park Avenue, New York, N.Y. 10016
Distributed in Australia by Capricorn Book Co. Pty. Ltd.
Unit 5C1 Lincoln St., Lane Cove, N.S.W. 2066
Distributed in the United Kingdom by Blandford Press
Link House, West Street, Poole, Dorset BH15 1LL, England
Distributed in Canada by Oak Tree Press Ltd.
℅ Canadian Manda Group, P.O. Box 920, Station U
Toronto, Ontario, Canada M8Z 5P9
Manufactured in the United States of America

Contents

Preface

So you want to buy a home?

Congratulations! Your investment in this book puts you way ahead of the competition in your quest for information before making the biggest purchase of your life. There is no need to expend time and money on eight or nine books in the separate fields of appraising, financing, interest rates, the economy, brokerage practices and law, or tax accounting. This book amalgamates all the interdisciplinary information into one source. You can meet with all the experts at *your* leisure—they are at your fingertips!

How to Buy a Home While You Can Still Afford To takes the mumbo-jumbo and confusion out of home buying! It is full of practical information for you: how to compute your taxes as a renter versus income taxes saved if you own; avoiding legal problems with contracts and mortgages; how to utilize a wide variety of financing vehicles to your best advantage; how to shop for a mortgage; and how to pick the right neighborhood and home. The book contains useful checklists to help you avoid making any major blunders in the home-buying process. Let your competitors make the mistakes!

The author is grateful to the following people who have contributed to this book: Rennard Strickland, Jim O'Neill, Woody, Holly, Lauren, Robb, Bill Burch, Elio, Artie, Damaise, Bernie, Jeff, Larry Rausch at Maday Mortgage Co., Leslie, Brian, Kevin, Susan, Chuck, Mrs. K. Bosnik, Charles Nurnberg, Calvin Hall and Langston University, Ron, Shelley, McCummiskey and Reed Realtors, Bob Bagler, and my doctors, Boles, Ruff, Wall and O'Toole.

Special thanks to my brother Tim for research assistance, and to Jerome and Mary Jane Murphy, who have been the author's best and most loved teachers.

1
Why Has the Cost of Homes Skyrocketed?

Stories in the newspapers and on television have scared the heck out of many potential home buyers.

". . . and the cost of the average new home is now over $102,000 nationally. Few families earn enough to afford today's new homes. Some economists expect prices to double or triple in the next ten years. Bear Phillips is next with sports news, as Happy Talk News 7 continues. . . ."

Is the American Dream a cruel hoax? Can you still acquire one of the fruits of freedom, namely a home of your own? Or has the price of your dream become too prohibitive?

The notion that there are no decent homes for people with modest incomes is nonsense!

Need some reassurance?

Let's take a few minutes to analyze some numbers. First, understand that the $102,000 price tag refers to only *new* homes. Second, that $102,000 figure is an *average*. So, obviously some new homes cost more than the average figure, and some cost less.

The *median* price of new homes is near $84,000 as of January 1986.

So far, we have been talking only about *new* homes, and statistics related to new homes. What about older or *existing* homes? In 1984 over 2.8 million existing homes were sold, and in 1985 over 3 million changed hands. Forecasters predict sales of perhaps 40 million units from 1985--1995. Wow! That's a lot of existing homes for sale, and they come in all sizes, prices and areas.

Let's look at some more stats—you'll be pleasantly surprised. As of late 1985 the median sales price of existing homes was $76,500. But 10.9 percent of all existing homes sold were priced under $40,000 with another 9.2 percent in the $40,000 to $50,000 range. The $50,000 to $60,000 market totalled another 11.2 percent.

Although the median-priced existing home was $76,500 in late 1985, regional prices varied. In the Northeast, the median price was $89,800; whereas it was only $60,800 in the Midwest; the figure for the South was $76,000; and $93,100 was the median price in the West.

Let me make a crucial point here: Real estate markets are essentially *local* in nature, with each town experiencing different supply/demand conditions.

Let me demonstrate to you how prices vary in different regions of the nation. The National Association of Realtors has kept statistics on the sales of existing homes for the past few years.

For example, as of June 1985, in the Northeast area 6.5 percent of sales were priced under $40,000, with another 6.9 percent in the $40,000 to $50,000 range. In the South, 9.9 percent were under $40,000, and 10.1 percent were priced between $40,000 and $50,000. There's good news for those who live in the Midwest region of the country with 10.1 percent under $30,000, then 11 percent between $30,000 and $40,000, and another 13.5 percent in the $40,000 to $50,000 range. If you live in the West, the picture is a bit more grim: only 2.5 percent of sales were under $40,000, with 3.7 percent more in the $40,000 to $50,000 bracket. Why is this? Homes, lots, and demand are larger. Chapter 7 explains how you can get this info from realtors and local sources to determine price ranges for your town.

Although real estate markets are essentially local in nature, there are national factors that affect local markets. As such, these factors might influence your investment plans, and, therefore, deserve your attention.

Let's briefly examine the major supply-and-demand factors.

CONSTRUCTION COSTS

One of the major factors contributing to the spiralling cost of *new* homes is rising construction costs. And these rising costs are reflected in the sales prices, as builders pass the costs on to buyers.

A wide variety of materials go into the building of a new home.

There are bricks, lumber, paint, plastics, metals, concrete products, heating and cooling equipment, plumbing fixtures, and many more items.

During good years in the business cycle, the rise in construction costs is greater than the rise in consumer prices. A variance from this relationship occurs in 1970, 1974–'75, and 1979–'81, reflecting recession and a housing slump. The following table confirms this data.

Percentage Change in Residential Construction Costs and Consumer Prices

Year	Residential Construction	Consumer Prices
1950	5.5	1.0
1955	3.0	− 0.4
1960	1.6	1.6
1965	3.2	1.7
1970	5.4	5.9
1971	8.5	4.3
1972	9.8	3.4
1973	9.2	6.2
1974	8.1	11.0
1975	6.7	9.1
1976	8.2	5.8
1977	9.0	6.5
1978	9.0	7.7
1979	9.1	11.3
1980	8.3	13.5
1981	5.5	10.4
1982	8.5	6.1
1983	5.9	3.2
1984	5.7	4.3

Sources: E. H. Boeckh and Associates, Department of Labor, and United States League of Savings Associations.

It takes men, money, materials, and land to build homes. The services of many tradesmen are required for buildings. Many of the trades are dominated by union policies and wages. Oftentimes, wage structures are tied to increases in the cost of living. Do *you* think the wages of plumbers, electricians, carpenters, roofers, landscapers, etc. will go down in the years ahead? I don't.

Builders have to borrow money at current interest rates to finance their ventures. This expense is passed on to home buyers. There is a table in a later chapter with a history of interest rates, showing that the high cost of borrowed capital is here to stay.

COSTS AFFECT EXISTING HOMES

As of early 1986, new homes cost about $50 a square foot to build. The figure varies in different areas, and with features the home includes. What becomes of those who desire homes, but can't afford new ones? They buy existing homes.

As the cost to build new homes rises, the replacement cost of older homes rises, too! The market price of older homes rises, provided they are in desirable areas.

Consider, too, the *improvements* people make in their homes. Americans are a nation of do-it-yourselfers. Bathrooms and kitchens are remodelled, yards are landscaped, central air-conditioning is installed, homes are insulated, rooms are added, etc. The materials needed to make these improvements cost more. These improvements in the quality of older homes increase their market values.

LAND VALUES

Land in desirable areas appreciates. Land that no one wants may decline in value. Nationwide, we have experienced steadily increasing values. Remember, the market value of real estate is local in nature.

As the saying goes—land is a valuable commodity; they aren't making any more of it!

POPULATION TRENDS

The baby-boom generation, those people born from 1946–1966, will fuel the housing demand through 1995. The younger boomers will be entering their prime home-buying ages. The older boomers will be in their 40s and heading for age 50. Because incomes tend to peak around age 45, and about two-thirds of married women between ages 35 and 45 now work, the aging boomer families will have plenty of income. And I predict that they will spend a lot of that income on larger homes with more amenities. The "trade-up" sales market should really boom!

MOBILITY

Americans are on the move! Machines, money, and our adventurous spirit have made American society very mobile. Estimates show that one of five families moves every year.

Where is everyone going? Across town? Out of town? Into your city? To the suburbs? Back to nature? To new jobs in the Sun Belt? To areas with safer, better schools? I guess you know whether your area is experiencing growth or not. Federally financed highways, new shopping centers, and economic opportunities contribute significantly to population shifts.

THE ECONOMY

The nation's economic health affects local real estate markets. Higher disposable personal income means people have more money to save or spend on whatever they desire. The availability of money greatly influences lenders in your area. They influence builders, who influence you.

GOVERNMENTAL ACTIONS

Don't ever underestimate Washington D.C.'s influence over your local real estate market. Changes in the tax laws can leave you less disposable income. The Federal Reserve Board can make money flow like beer on Saint Patrick's Day. The Fed can also turn the printing presses off.

Studies suggest that federal and local regulations have added 20 percent and more to the price tag of new homes. One builder told me that most of the pre-World War II homes would not meet today's standards and codes, and therefore would not be built.

Local laws have a big effect on new construction. Zoning laws, limited or no-growth policies, building codes, etc., all must be considered by developers and builders. Last, but perhaps most important, will inflation cause a continued loss in the dollar's purchasing power? (Inflation is an excessive increase in the money supply that is not merited by a corresponding increase in goods and services produced.)

BOOM TO BUST: HOUSING 1978–1982

The housing industry went from feast to famine over this five-year period. The first year, 1978, was a great year in housing! Four million existing homes were sold, with a median price of $48,700. At the same time, 1½ million new homes were under construction, with a median price of $55,700. Housing was affordable at 9 percent conventional interest rates. Real estate achieved Nirvana because a variety of factors made home ownership an attractive investment.

First, buyers received *positive leverage* on the funds they borrowed at 9 percent as homes appreciated at an annual average of 14 percent. Second, interest rates were low in "real" (inflation-adjusted) terms. Third, Federal income tax regulations encouraged home ownership. Fourth, regulation of thrifts limited interest rates that could be paid to savers, thus subsidizing housing at the expense of the small saver. Fifth, loans and housing were affordable for median- and lower-income families. In 1978, first-time buyers were involved in about half of all home sales. The ratio of monthly payments to monthly income was below the 30 percent level.

Then housing sales weakened in late 1979 and continued to slump. By 1982, only 1.9 million existing homes were sold, plus 396,000 new homes. This tailspin was labelled a depression in housing. The cause of this tailspin can be best analyzed by focusing upon the reversal of four of the above five factors.

First of all, leverage turned negative, as the following numbers reveal.

Leverage in Housing (1978–1982)

	1978	1979	1980	1981	1982[1]
Interest Rate[2]	9.37	10.59	12.46	14.39	15.00
Housing Appreciation[3]	14.00	14.90	12.00	5.60	3.00
Leverage	+4.63	+4.31	−.46	−8.79	−12.00

1. Estimated.
2. Interest rate on all mortgages, Federal Home Loan Bank Board Journal, January 1983, Table S.5.1, page 56.
3. Appreciation estimated from U.S. Bureau of the Census, Federal Home Loan Bank Board, National Association of Realtors.

REAL INTEREST RATES

Real interest rates reflect rate of return after inflation is considered. From 1950 through 1975, real interest rates averaged about 3 percent. The period from 1978 through 1982 saw fluctuating real interest rates, thanks to unexpected levels of inflation.

Real Interest Rates on Home Mortgages (1978–1982)

	1978	1979	1980	1981	1982[1]
Interest Rate[2]	9.37	10.59	12.46	14.39	15.00
Inflation[3]	7.70	11.30	13.50	10.40	3.90
Real Interest Rate	+1.67	−.71	−1.04	+3.99	+11.10

1. Estimated.
2. Interest rate on all mortgages, Federal Home Loan Bank Board Journal, January 1983, Table S.5.1, page 56.
3. Inflation as measured by the CPI on a year-to-year basis, Bureau of Labor Statistics.

DEREGULATION OF THRIFTS

Interest rate ceilings on interest rates payable to savers are being gradually phased out through 1986. Because institutions have to pay more to attract funds, they have to charge more to borrowers. Regulatory changes also allow lenders to offer adjustable interest rate loans now, thus shifting some of the risk of inflation to the borrower.

AFFORDABILITY—A BIG PROBLEM

Interest rates on conventional loans averaged 9.5 percent in 1978. In 1979 rates were 10.75 percent, in 1980 they increased to 12.65 percent, soared to 14.75 percent in 1981, and topped 15 percent in 1982. Rising interest rates meant that fewer buyers had the income necessary to qualify for loans, as monthly payments soared. In 1978 monthly payments averaged about $400. By 1981 this figure flew above the $800 mark. With a 25 percent qualifying ratio, a buyer needed a gross income above $38,000 a year to meet the average monthly payment of $800.

First-time buyers were reduced to only 13 percent of those buying homes in 1981. Financing patterns were altered. In 1976 only 10 percent of home sales utilized seller financing, but by 1981 almost half of all sales involved creative financing.

TAX FACTORS STILL REMAIN FAVORABLE

Favorable income tax treatment afforded homeowners continued to make housing an attractive investment for some, even in the 1979–1982 slide. Because homeowners are allowed to deduct mortgage interest and property taxes from their gross incomes, they pay tax on less adjusted income, plus they are lowered into a less progressive tax bracket. These items allowed homeowners to save $31 billion in Federal income taxes in 1981, according to a Congressional Budget Office study. This figure could climb to $82 billion by 1986.

THE HOUSING MARKET RECOVERS

After a dismal 1982, with only 1.9 million existing homes and about 400,000 new homes sold, the housing market rebounded in 1983. Fueling the resurgence was a hefty drop in interest rates from the 16 percent range to 12¾ percent. There were 2.7 million existing homes and 623,000 new homes sold. Interest rates of 12½ percent in 1984 produced sales of 2.86 million existing homes and 639,000 new homes. An even better year was 1985, as interest rates hovered near 12 percent. Estimated sales figures were above the 3 million mark for existing homes, and new home sales were near the 650,000 mark.

The affordability dilemma was eased by lower interest rates. Recall that in 1982 the annual income needed to qualify for a median-priced home hit the $38,000 level. By late 1985, this income mark dropped to $29,600. Falling interest rates also improved the leverage and real interest-rate factors.

It should be obvious that the housing industry is cyclical, and very sensitive to macroeconomic conditions, especially changes in interest rates. The lessons learned from observing this cycle are valid and applicable to any given year.

HOUSING AS AN APPRECIATING ASSET

One of the factors fueling the demand for housing has been the attractiveness of the single-family home as an investment. The following table gives you some historical perspective on housing appreciation.

Median Prices of Homes (1970–1984)

	Median Price	
Year	New Homes	Existing Homes
1970	$23,400	$23,000
1971	25,200	24,800
1972	27,600	26,700
1973	32,500	28,900
1974	35,900	32,000
1975	39,300	35,300
1976	44,200	38,100
1977	48,800	42,900
1978	55,700	48,700
1979	62,900	55,700
1980	64,600	62,200
1981	68,900	66,400
1982	69,300	67,800
1983	75,300	70,300
1984	79,900	72,400

Sources: Bureau of the Census and National Association of Realtors.

BYE-BYE TO THE AMERICAN PIE?

Is the home-buying game over? Did you miss your slice? NO!! The risks are higher and the return is no longer automatic. Nonetheless, the knowledgeable buyer will get a hefty piece of the American Dream. Rewards await the well-informed, so read on!

2
Why Americans Own

A look around your town may reveal some lavish $100,000-plus homes. Certainly, $50,000 homes are a common sight in America. If you are a non-homeowner, this can really blow your mind! You want to get your piece of the action before costs soar out of sight.

Odds are you grew up in a home that your folks owned, but let us view ownership in time and place perspectives. In feudal England, the King had title to all lands, and parcelled them out to his lords. In return, the lords placed their armies at the King's disposal. The common man "rented" land from the lords, paying the lords with crops and services (like serving in the army).

If you were one of the younger sons of a feudal farmer, you might never have received your own land to farm. Those of you readers who are just married can imagine how thrilling it must have been to share a shack with your spouse and the rest of your family.

Although private property was sanctioned by the early colonists, our young nation required another essential ingredient—capital! Americans formed voluntary savings clubs to make loans. Because the government kept its hands out of the citizens' pockets, savings grew and were invested.

Prior to the 1930s, loans were both favorable and unfavorable, when compared to today's real estate financing terms. Big down payments, such as 50 percent, were common. Rarely did a loan term exceed five years! On the other hand, costs and interest rates were lower. You didn't have bureaucrats setting regulations. Zoning was unconstitutional until the 1920s. (No one could vote to determine that the first story of your home must be brick, or that your lot must be such and such a size, etc.). Even in 1890, 48 percent of the housing was owner-occupied.

The Depression of the 1930s hit people with home loans hard, because if they had no jobs, they couldn't make the payments. Foreclosures abounded. The federal government took steps to remedy this and since then has expanded its participation in the residential real estate market. However, the notion that the government was the savior for the housing industry, or the entire economy, for that matter, is a fallacy.

We are fortunate to be able to enjoy the fruits of freedom, and hopefully we can pass it on to generations of unborn Americans. That's why I included this historical material in the book.

THE AMERICAN WAY OF LIFE

Ingrained in our culture is the tradition of home ownership. The fact that many immigrants never owned land in the country of their birth contributed to the desire to own land. It was symbolic of "making it" in America. Today, too, we still exhibit that pride in ownership! Ownership feeds the ego. Your personality is expressed through your choice of ownership. People judge you by the neighborhood you live in, the furnishings in your home, and other external signs of your level in life. A bit sad, but true.

Many of us have grown up in homes owned by our parents. We've grown accustomed to this lifestyle. Young buyers often expect to buy a home that has all the same luxuries they grew up with, such as central air-conditioning, radar ranges, dishwashers, recreation rooms, big yards, and 1,500 or more square feet of living area. (The median new home of 1980 is roughly double the size of those built right after World War II.) But remember, it took your parents a few years to earn the salaries and acquire assets to buy that home. Today, you will probably make monthly payments of at least $500 for such luxuries.

Homes offer a lifestyle that is not available in apartments. Privacy is a big factor. Homes have yards for entertaining friends at a cookout and keeping the kids busy. Mom has her garden. The pets have a place to roam. Dad can have his workshop in the basement or garage. The increased enjoyment is limited only by the imagination.

THE HOME IS YOUR BEST SAVINGS ACCOUNT

Why is this so? Because you force yourself to save the rent you used to spend. Now you pay rent to yourself. Your monthly payments are in effect a monthly savings plan. (Something that was missing when you collected rent receipts from your landlord!)

As your equity (or ownership) in your home builds up and values rise in your area, you can borrow money easily, using your home equity as collateral. Home equity is usually the single biggest savings account that people have. Perhaps you have noticed the ads that suggest you "Make your home work for you," or "Ask your home for a new car!"

THE HOME IS A GOOD INVESTMENT

Taxes and interest are deductions from gross income when figuring your federal income tax. The home is also a good hedge against inflation. It protects the owner from higher rents and higher building costs. Since the early 1970s, real estate has outperformed most forms of investment. It offers above-average appreciation, and high leverage.

REASONS PEOPLE DO NOT OWN

The biggest disadvantage of home ownership is that maintenance and repairs cost time and money. Some people are physically unable to keep a house up, others just hate to do the work. Some Americans are afraid of big mortgages! They pale at the thought of thirty-year debts and having that hang over their heads. Americans hate debt.

Homeownership 1890–1983

Year	Occupied Units	Owner- occupied Units	Renter- occupied Units	Percent- age Owned	Percent- age Rented
1890	12,690,000	6,066,000	6,624,000	47.8	52.2
1900	15,964,000	7,455,000	8,509,000	46.7	53.3
1910	20,256,000	9,301,000	10,955,000	45.9	54.1
1920	24,352,000	11,114,000	13,238,000	45.6	54.4
1930	29,905,000	14,280,000	15,625,000	47.8	52.2
1940	34,855,000	15,196,000	19,659,000	43.6	56.4
1950	42,826,000	23,560,000	19,266,000	55.0	45.0
1960	53,024,000	32,797,000	20,227,000	61.9	38.1
1970	63,445,000	39,886,000	23,559,000	62.9	37.1
1975	72,523,000	46,867,000	25,656,000	64.6	35.4
1980	80,390,000	51,795,000	28,595,000	64.4	35.6
1983	84,638,000	54,724,000	29,914,000	64.7	35.3

Source: Bureau of the Census and United States League of Savings Associations.

3
Can the Bubble Burst?

The question I am asked most frequently is "How long do you think this rapid escalation of home prices will continue?" A bust in the real estate market is the biggest fear of purchasers and would-be purchasers, who worry about dizzying price levels. This fear is voiced in many ways: How high is high? When will it all stop? It has to end somewhere! This is too good to be true! Is there any end in sight? Will prices drop? It can't go on forever!

Because of the demographic and other factors advanced in the previous chapters, demand will exceed supply of housing nationwide for the decade. Naturally some areas and communities will be more desirable than others and command higher prices. However, let me caution you—there is a joker in the deck! The joker is the federal government. There is a danger in merely stating that demand is bullish in the 1980s for housing (or for clothing, calculators, and Frisbees for that matter!), without considering the general macro-economic environment for the decade.

GOVERNMENT AND INFLATION: THE HIDDEN TAX

There is a very real threat of even more rapidly accelerating inflation playing havoc with the American economy and eventually resulting in the complete destruction of the dollar as we know it, followed by depression. Inflation is a *money disease,* caused by the production of unearned dollars by the government. Inflation is a *tax* upon existing dollars. Inflation buys votes—because it is used to paper over deficit spending and pay for government giveaways. With over one-half of all Americans now dependent upon the federal government for a check, it is doubtful whether this deliberate destruction of the dollar will end voluntarily. Since raising taxes to pay for these giveaways is unpopular, the government will probably continue to tax in a subtle way—through inflation!

Current economic signs that should disturb you include: record levels of indebtedness by both government and consumers; liberal reserve requirements for banks; low or no productivity increases nationwide; an F.D.I.C. fund that could cover only 1½ percent of total deposits should the banks run upon hard times; and the continued erosion of your dollar's purchasing power.

HOMEOWNERS ARE SAFER THAN RENTERS

You are probably better off to be a *homeowner* than a renter in troubled times, provided you are not in an area that could be wrecked by social disorder. In inflationary periods, you will be paying off your mortgage in cheaper dollars! (That is, dollars that have less purchasing power than those that you originally borrowed.)

Your payments on principal and interest will normally remain fixed throughout the life of the loan, or be limited to small increases. (More about financing later.) But if inflation starts to trot and then gallop, odds are good that you will receive increases in your salary, presuming you are still working. If inflation really goes berserk, you will be paid gobs of paper, and perhaps that monthly paycheck will be enough to pay off the entire mortgage!

But wouldn't renters pay off landlords in cheaper dollars too? Yes, but monthly rents will probably rise as inflation does; however, fixed monthly principal and interest payments to a lender by a homeowner do not rise. (A variable rate mortgage is an exception to the rule, but increases in the rate are strictly limited and would make no difference essentially in hyper-inflationary times.)

What about rent controls? Wouldn't local governments attempt to freeze rents in a period of trouble, just as they have done in the past? Yes, they probably would: Since one out of three people rent, there are a lot of votes out there and tenants outnumber landlords! The long-term results of such rent controls are always disastrous. Landlords are faced with rising operating costs, but their revenues are not rising. There are little or no reserves for major repairs, especially if the property is highly financed. Eventually properties decline, and are unloaded on the lender or the government. You don't want to be stuck in a place that is deteriorating.

THE HOMEOWNER'S VOTE COUNTS

Let me also point out that two out of three Americans live in their own home! They represent an even bigger voting bloc than renters. Suppose unemployment grows rapidly and people are having trouble paying their mortgages and bills. It is doubtful that the government will allow widespread foreclosures, because where would these people go? A legislative holiday or short-term moratorium on overdue mortgage payments is the likely government response. Of course, such action would further incapacitate the lenders, and all the savers who contributed funds to the lender. (Your savings? Your parents? Your insurance company? Your pension plan?)

Suppose there are less serious economic problems: there are no rent controls, but you are laid off your job. Should you rent or own? Is it worse to miss a rent payment or a mortgage payment? Probably a rent payment, because the landlord has more to lose than a lender, who can always attach the collateral or security (your home) for satisfaction of the debt. Landlords are apt to evict tenants in a hurry, and replace them with new sources of revenue. Besides, the homeowner has time on his side! Lenders do not like to foreclose; it takes time, lawyers, and energy. Most states even provide grace periods for borrowers to redeem their equity prior to foreclosure. This grace period may run six months! A renter does not have this cushion. There is more safety in home ownership in bad times!

USE A HOME TO BEAT INFLATION

How can you pinpoint the beginning of a monetary collapse and the resulting bust in real estate and other industries? No one is positive. Personally, I feel that if inflation hits 25 to 30 percent, with unemployment above 10 percent, that could be the psychological point of no return. If we ever reach such an inflation rate, you would be in the safest position if you had your home paid in full. If your home is still mortgaged, you'd be better off to be highly mortgaged. Don't let your equity sit in your house doing nothing! Why? Because it could dry up fast if there is a deflation, and also because you should use it to invest in inflation beaters. (Best bets: gold, silver, and hard currencies like the Swiss franc or German mark.)

Have I scared the heck out of you? My only reason for including this material in the book is to meet people's fears head-on. Brokers don't like to talk "bust" with prospective buyers, nor do lenders (because they might be out of a job, too!). Actually, talking frankly about these fears can only lead to a realization of the merits of home ownership, and a bright broker would point this out to prospective buyers!

Relax and read on—you are going to get that home!

4
Should I Wait for Interest Rates to Drop?

Interest rates may be defined simply as the cost of using somebody else's money for a certain period of time. People may desire to borrow money for a short time, such as a builder who needs to borrow a large sum of money for six to nine months to finance the construction of a new home. Others, such as yourself and other home buyers who want thirty-year loans, desire to borrow money for a long time.

Because there is a different market (supply/demand structure) for short-term and long-term loans, the interest rates are different, too. Different terminology exists to identify the different interest rates.

The "prime rate" is a phrase you hear on the evening news quite often. It is a short-term interest rate that banks will charge their best customers who can offer sound assets to pledge as security for the short-term loan. The prime rate when Ford left office in early 1977 was 6¾ percent. As Carter left office in early 1981, the prime rate was over 20 percent, and as of October 1985 was 9½ percent.

So what, you ask? Home builders watch the prime rate, as their construction loans are short-term, and normally cost prime plus 2–3 percent. This means that as of October 1985, builders must pay 12 percent interest. That is expensive, especially if the house does not sell for eight or ten months after completion and the builder is still paying debt service.

"Mortgage rates" are long-term interest rates charged to the home buyer who pledges his home as security. (This will be *you*!) We will focus our attention on these interest rates, and, from this point on in your reading, interest rates will refer to mortgage rates unless specified otherwise.

WHAT DETERMINES INTEREST RATES?

To put it succinctly, the supply of money available to be loaned out and the demand for that money determine interest rates.

Demand is fairly easy to understand, in general terms: As interest rates rise, the demand for these higher rates drops.

Analysis of supply is more complicated. Where do lenders get their money? Obvious sources are depositors, loan payments made to them, revenues from their investments, and money market certificates purchased from them. Why should you care how lenders such as savings and loan associations get their funds? Because—you need to understand interest rates!

FINANCIAL INTERMEDIARIES

Thrift institutions are intermediaries (or brokers) that provide a place for borrowers and lenders to meet. You are probably both! In the eyes of the institution, you are a lender by virtue of your savings and checking accounts. You may be a borrower. Have you had a car loan? A student loan? Do you want a home loan?

Are these institutions a bunch of greedy people who arbitrarily set interest rates at their whim? Are they gouging you by charging 13 percent interest for a thirty-year home loan? Contrary to the impression created by some economically illiterate television writers, the answer is NO! For example, in 1984 savings and loan associations paid savers an average of 10.14 percent on their various accounts, which means that funds *cost* them 10.14 percent. That same year, the average interest rate charged on conventional loans was 12.37 percent. That figure represents a 2.23 percent interest rate above what they paid for the money.

In my opinion, that's a reasonable spread or brokerage fee, considering that the broker/intermediary runs the risk of loan defaults, foreclosures, and the erosion of the dollar's value over a thirty-year loan term due to inflation. For the unconvinced reader, observe the following data on page 23.

REGULATION OF THRIFTS

Savings and loan associations are the largest single source of residential mortgage loans, supplying over half of the total supply of funds. For years, the government regulated the interest rates that savings and loan associations could pay to attract savers. This artificially low rate guaranteed them a "cheap" supply of funds to loan home buyers. Savers were subsidizing American housing. By the late 1970s, legislative changes allowed savings and loan associations to make adjustable-rate loans, thus shifting some of the inflation

Average Cost of Funds versus Mortgage Rates

Year	Savings Deposits in FSLIC-insured Savings Institutions	Year	Conventional Loans on New Homes, Effective Interest Rate
1965	4.23%	1965	5.81%
1970	5.06	1970	8.45
1971	5.33	1971	7.74
1972	5.39	1972	7.60
1973	5.55	1973	7.96
1974	5.98	1974	8.92
1975	6.24	1975	9.00
1976	6.32	1976	9.00
1977	6.41	1977	9.02
1978	6.52	1978	9.56
1979	7.31	1979	10.78
1980	8.69	1980	12.66
1981	10.70	1981	14.70
1982	11.03	1982	15.14
1983	10.03	1983	12.66
1984*	10.14	1984	12.37

*Preliminary.
Sources: Federal Deposit Insurance Corporation; Federal Home Loan Bank Board; Federal Reserve Board; United States League of Savings Institutions.

risk to the borrower, and also approved the gradual phasing out of ceilings on interest rates payable to depositors.

THE ROLE OF THE FED

Think of the Fed as the "Banker's Bank"! Your local bank can borrow money through the Federal Reserve system. The Fed charges a "discount rate" of interest.

Basically, the Fed's job is to regulate the supply of money existing in the United States! The Fed controls the growth or contraction of the money supply in three basic ways: 1) by adjusting the discount rate to borrowing banks; 2) by adjusting the reserve requirements for banks, which controls the ultimate amount of funds a bank must keep on hand or loan out at a given period of time; 3) by buying and selling securities in the open market, which determines the amount of funds available at any given time for borrowing.

Have you heard the phrase "tighten the money supply"? It refers to a policy of the Fed to slow or decrease growth of the money supply, utilizing one or all of the three ways described above. Such a policy normally results in less money available to be loaned out, and leads to higher interest rates as competing borrowers fight for loans and bid higher interest rates (rents for the use of money). As we learned in Chapter 1, such a policy, if coupled with fiscal restraint, would curb inflation.

Correspondingly, a "loose money" policy results in an increase in the money supply and leads initially to lower interest rates. If the increase is too large, it will lead to higher inflation and higher interest rates in the long run.

FUTURE INTEREST RATES

Long-run predictions about the housing market are very hard to make, because its health is linked so closely to general macroeconomic conditions. The best I can do for you is to present my *opinion* on the most probable scenario for housing, and to highlight possible trends.

On the national economic front, sustained growth through 1990 is possible, but it is most likely that this growth will be marked by one mild recession. The big question mark is the Federal Reserve Board. Can the Fed stay within its targeted growth rates for money? If so, interest rates in the 9–13 percent range are plausible bets through 1990. With many blaming our trade deficit woes on the "strong" dollar, the Fed may be tempted to loosen the money supply in hopes of driving down the value of the dollar. I believe that the dollar is properly valued because it is freely traded, and attempts by the Fed to weaken the dollar will lead to higher inflation and higher interest rates. The 1986 and 1988 elections will determine to a large extent voter opinion on monetary policy, and how policy should be conducted in the late 1980s. Should loose-money advocates prevail, look for an inflationary burst, followed by stagnation and rising interest rates.

The homeowner's tax benefits seem safe from tax reform, although the depreciation allowance for investors could be trimmed.

I do not believe federal budget deficits will be as big a problem as most observers think, because the most important factor is the size of the budget, not the size of the deficits. The public sector is crowded out by *any* government spending, be it financed by borrowing or by taxes. On the bright side, President Reagan has slowed the growth of the federal budget significantly, and I expect this to continue. This will increase savings, helping to supply the funds for loans.

A VALUABLE LESSON

We have had twenty-eight recessions since the Civil War, averaging one about every four years. Despite all the political bluster, we cannot recession-proof the economy, because we are not even sure what causes the business cycle. No one can predict when the next downturn will come nor how prolonged it will be. We can expect housing to react characteristically in both the recession and recovery stages of the business cycle.

Remember, the housing cycle endures.

Remember, too, that even if interest rates drop, home prices may continue to rise in the 12–15 percent yearly range. You could wait for a drop in rates, but this could be more than offset by rising prices, higher down payments, and higher monthly payments.

To help you understand this trade-off, consider the following examples.

THE RATE IS RIGHT

How often have you heard someone say, "We were thinking about buying a home right now, but my husband says the interest rates are too high at the moment; so we'll wait!" (Perhaps your parents heard the same line after World War II when interest rates were too high at 4 percent!) Waiting for lower interest rates can be a very risky and very costly strategy. Witness this sad vignette:

Randall and Paula Shupe *almost* made up their minds to buy a nice twenty-year-old, two-bedroom home for $35,000. They qualified for a thirty-year, 90 percent conventional loan at 10½ percent interest. Paula's economics instructor predicted a drop in the interest rate, based upon the leading economic indicators. Paula convinced Randy it was smart to wait—after all, she reasoned, a ½ percent interest drop would save them a lot on monthly payments on their loan.

The Shupes waited, and, sure enough, one year later the inter-

Concurrent Effects of Value and Interest Rate

Rise in Value	Price	Interest Rate (%)	10% Down Payment	Loan Amount	*Monthly Payment	Total Payments (30 years— 360 mos.)
ORIGINAL BASE	$35,000	10½	$3,500	$31,500	$288	$103,680
10% rise	$38,500	10	$3,850	$34,650	$304	$109,440
15% rise	$40,250	10	$4,025	$36,225	$318	$114,480
10% rise	$38,500	9½	$3,850	$34,650	$291	$104,760
15% rise	$40,250	9½	$4,025	$36,225	$304	$109,440
Suppose you wait, and interest rates never drop!						
10% rise	$38,500	11	$3,850	$34,650	$330	$118,800
15% rise	$40,250	11	$4,025	$36,225	$345	$124,200
10% rise	$38,500	11½	$3,850	$34,650	$343	$123,480
15% rise	$40,250	11½	$4,025	$36,225	$363	$130,680

* Monthly payment includes payment on principal and interest only. (Escrow payments for taxes and insurance are not included!)

est rate had come down ½ percent. "Let's buy now!" urged Paula. But the Shupes discovered that homes had appreciated 15 percent in their area. That $35,000 home now cost $40,250!! Instead of a $3,500 down payment, they now need $4,025; and their monthly payments on principal and interest have increased from $288 a month to $318. Under the same qualification standards used by the lender, the Shupes would have to be making about $120 more a month now to qualify. If the Shupes held the mortgage for thirty years, over that term they would pay $10,800 more at this "lower rate."

In inflationary markets, delays always raise your initial costs, and usually negate any savings you might enjoy from lower interest rate movements. (Incidentally, when you read this book, the interest rates used in this example may be too high or too low in relation to your time frame. Fear not, the lesson to be learned is valid at any rate.)

Take a few minutes to study the chart on page 26. I want you to be able to construct your own chart for your own situation. See for yourself just how costly delays can become, and observe the trade-offs involved.

CLOSING COMMENTS

A few final remarks are in order before we close the Chapter. Remember that as your monthly payments rise, as indicated in the following trade-off table, so too must your monthly income in order to meet the lender's qualifications. (Probably you will need a rise in income of four times the rise in monthly payments!)

Study the following chart, which shows you home mortgage interest rates over the years. It will sharpen your perspective!

Interest Rates on Conventional Loans

Year	Rate (%)	Year	Rate (%)
1965	5¾	1976	9
1966	6¼	1977	9¼
1967	6½	1978	9¾
1968	7	1979	10¾
1969	7¾	1980	12¾
1970	8½	1981	14½
1971	7¾	1982	15¼
1972	7½	1983	12¾
1973	8	1984	12½
1974	8¾	1985	12¼
1975	9		

5

Tax Advantages of Home Ownership

Did you know that you will have a lower federal income tax by owning your own home? Your mortgage interest and property taxes are itemized deductions from your gross income. Because your gross income is lowered, your income tax is also lowered.

Let's work an example together!

Suppose Richard Sherman earns $20,000 a year. He and his wife Karen, and little baby Zeke, live in a south Chicago apartment complex. The Shermans want to buy a $40,000 home, and a lending officer has assured them they can qualify for a 90 percent conventional loan at 11 percent interest for thirty years. Assume the property taxes on this $40,000 home will be $700 per year.

We can compute the first year's entire interest expense in the following manner:

(1) $40,000 × .90 = $36,000 loan amount.

(2) $36,000 × .11 interest rate = $3,960 interest for year 1.

Add $3,960 plus the $700 property tax for a total of $4,660 in deductions.

If the Shermans owned that $40,000 home, they would have $4,660 in deductions as computed above. Subtract $4,660 from a gross income of $20,000, and you will get a taxable income of $15,340. This lowers the Shermans to a lesser tax bracket. Specifically, their income tax would be $1,493.

Finally, look at the difference ownership makes!

$2,511   (income tax if they continue to rent)

−1,493   (income tax if they own)

$1,018   tax savings by owning.

Isn't that nice!

A worksheet is provided to help you compute your own tax advantage of home ownership.

Tax Savings Worksheet

(1) Your tax as a renter

enter here _____ (1)

Now, we follow these steps to find tax as an owner:

(2) Value of home × loan percentage = loan amount (a)

_____ × _____ = _____ (a)

(3) Loan amount (a) × interest rate = first year's interest (b)

_____ (a) × _____ = _____ (b)

(4) First year's interest (b) + property tax =

total deduction (c)

_____ (b) + _____ = _____ (c)

(5) Gross income − total deductions (c) = taxable income (d)

_____ − _____ (c) = _____ (d)

(6) Consult tax schedule rates, find the appropriate tax for your taxable income (d)

enter here _____ (6)

(7) Tax as a renter (1) − tax as an owner (6) = tax savings

_____ (1) − _____ (6) = _____

6

The Magic of Leverage

Leverage gives you a chance to multiply your gains by using a smaller initial investment. Real estate financing gives you great leverage. In essence, you can invest in a home for a down payment that is a fraction of the total purchase price.

The stock market once featured low down-payments (low "margins"), but the Depression of the 1930s toppled these paper castles. To buy stocks today, the margin is 80 percent of the purchase price. This is supposed to curb excessive speculation.

Let us investigate how leverage works for you in three forms of investment: savings accounts, the stock market, and residences.

Assume that you have $4,000 to invest.

SAVINGS ACCOUNT

If the $4,000 was put in a savings account that pays 5 percent interest, at the end of one year, your return would be $200 (a return of 5 percent on the initial investment). There is no leverage, because you need 100 percent of the $4,000 to make the initial investment. However, savings accounts are very safe; they require little or no management, and are very liquid.

BUYING STOCKS

Let us put the $4,000 in stocks. Assume the margin is 80 percent. With $4,000, we could buy $5,000 worth of stocks. Suppose the stocks we choose appreciate 5 percent in one year's time. We would get a return of $250, or 6¼ percent on the initial investment of $4,000. Here we see what a little leverage can do! We sowed only $4,000, but we reap the returns on $5,000.

"MONEY-MARKET CERTIFICATES"

Thrift institutions now offer savers six-month "money-market certificates," yielding interest that is a fraction below the rate which Treasury Bills return (9–13 percent over the past eighteen months). Normally they must be bought in $1,000 or larger denominations. These MMC's offer less liquidity (because you are penalized for early withdrawals), but higher returns than savings accounts. Suppose you invested in an MMC yielding 10 percent for an entire year; your $4,000 investment would return a little over $400 in interest.

BUYING A HOME

Now, let us invest the $4,000 in a home. Suppose we buy a $35,000 home, with a down payment of 10 percent, or $3,500, plus $500 in closing costs. Again, suppose the home appreciates only 5 percent in value over one year's time. Market value of our home would increase $1,750 ($35,000 × .05). That represents a return of 43.7 percent on our initial investment of $4,000. Financial leverage has multiplied our initial efforts (a $200 return) by 8.75 times!

Isn't that beautiful? Later on, we'll learn how to manipulate the financing terms, so our down payment may be less than 10 percent. We'll also learn how to pick a home that will appreciate more than 5 percent annually. In the past decade, appreciation of 10 percent or 15 percent, and even more, was quite normal in desirable areas!

The preceding examples were used merely to illustrate the effect leverage has on the rate of return. These simplistic examples are not meant to be an exhaustive study on the rates of return on comparative investments. The extremely sophisticated reader will recognize that there are ways to increase leverage in the stock market. For example, one could use options, warrants, or other tools.

Suffice it to say, leverage in the financing of real estate is a most attractive feature, one which few if any other forms of investment can match.

Understand, too, just as leverage multiplies your appreciation faster, it can also make you lose money faster if things go wrong. With the aid of this book, you will learn how to avoid a lemon and live happily ever after!

Before you start looking for a home to buy, it is important to know if you can afford one or not. You must know in what range you can afford to buy. I know that sounds simple, but I have run across a good number of people who are crushed when they find out that they cannot qualify for the needed loan amount.

Don't you make this mistake!

This Chapter will give you the necessary guidelines to decide for yourself. Of course you can always go to several lenders and get pre-qualified before you even go home-hunting.

In a later chapter, you will learn how and where to apply for a home loan. We'll cover loans and how to shop around in detail. But for now, I want you to merely get an idea of how much of a loan you can expect to get. Forget those old stories about buying a home at two and a half times your annual income. Forget about what the guy down the block told you!

Understand, first of all, that different lenders have slightly different rules that guide their thinking in home loans. Also, each lender, at different times, has a varying supply of money to lend. When money is "tight," the lender has fewer dollars to lend, and can be more choosy among those loan applicants who are competing for his money. If money is plentiful, the lender can stretch his guidelines in favor of you, the buyer.

Basically, supply-and-demand factors make up the local money markets that you will be dealing with.

I will list several criteria that you can rely on, with minimal deviation.

LOAN QUALIFICATION FORMULAS

Re: INCOME (1) for conventional loans: The buyer can afford monthly mortgage payments that are equal to 25 percent of gross monthly income. Gross income is the total before tax earnings of husband *and* wife; (2) for FHA loans: The buyer can afford payments equal to 20 percent of gross monthly income.

Re: DEBTS for all types of loans: The buyers' long-term debt cannot exceed one-third of monthly gross income of the family. Long-term debts are those that are six months or longer in length. (Example: car payments.) This one-third figure *includes* your proposed house payments.

All different types of loans are explained in later chapters. Also, these guidelines are slightly flexible, as each case is individually considered by the different lenders.

The following charts are designed to aid you in matching your monthly income with the approximate loan amount you could qualify for, providing you meet the debts criteria.

Loan Amount for Conventional Loans

Monthly Gross Income	Approximate Loan Amount	Monthly Gross Income	Approximate Loan Amount
500	12,500	1,240	31,000
520	13,000	1,280	32,000
560	14,000	1,320	33,000
600	15,000	1,360	34,000
640	16,000	1,400	35,000
680	17,000	1,440	36,000
720	18,000	1,480	37,000
760	19,000	1,520	38,000
800	20,000	1,560	39,000
840	21,000	1,600	40,000
880	22,000	1,800	45,000
920	23,000	2,000	50,000
960	24,000	2,200	55,000
1,000	25,000	2,400	60,000
1,040	26,000	2,600	65,000
1,080	27,000	2,800	70,000
1,120	28,000	3,000	75,000
1,160	29,000	3,200	80,000
1,200	30,000		

Loan Amount for FHA Loans

Monthly Gross Income	Approximate Loan Amount	Monthly Gross Income	Approximate Loan Amount
500	10,000	950	19,000
550	11,000	1,000	20,000
600	12,000	1,050	21,000
650	13,000	1,100	22,000
700	14,000	1,150	23,000
750	15,000	1,200	24,000
800	16,000	1,250	25,000
850	17,000	1,300	26,000
900	18,000	1,350	27,000

Loan Amount for FHA Loans (cont.)

Monthly Gross Income	Approximate Loan Amount	Monthly Gross Income	Approximate Loan Amount
1,400	28,000	2,300	46,000
1,450	29,000	2,350	47,000
1,500	30,000	2,400	48,000
1,550	31,000	2,450	49,000
1,600	32,000	2,500	50,000
1,650	33,000	2,550	51,000
1,700	34,000	2,600	52,000
1,750	35,000	2,650	53,000
1,800	36,000	2,700	54,000
1,850	37,000	2,750	55,000
1,900	38,000	2,800	56,000
1,950	39,000	2,850	57,000
2,000	40,000	2,900	58,000
2,050	41,000	2,950	59,000
2,100	42,000	3,000	60,000
2,150	43,000	3,250	65,000
2,200	44,000	3,500	70,000
2,250	45,000		

7
Selecting the Right Neighborhood

You don't start out looking for a home; you begin by looking for a neighborhood that will suit your lifestyle and meet your criteria. What if a Hugh Hefner-type mansion were located in one of three places: the middle of a Kansas wheatfield, the middle of a plush resort area, or the middle of an urban slum—which do *you* think would sell faster and at a higher price?

Chances are that you have lived in your present town for a while, and are familiar with the other neighborhoods in your town. You may also have relatives in the same town who can help point you toward an area you would like. But don't be blinded by subjective views! You should approach the home buying process in the same manner as a stranger to your area.

And what about a stranger to the area? Suppose you've been transferred to a different city. How do you analyze neighborhoods, especially when you have little or no first-hand information or experience?

There are four basic groups that will provide you with information about any area. These sources are: 1) homeowners in the neighborhood; 2) the business experts in the area; 3) collectors of economic data about the area; 4) professional real estate salespeople.

TALKING WITH HOMEOWNERS

The homeowner himself is sometimes the best source of information about the area. Drive through the entire area. Take a walk in the parks. Shop in the stores, and knock on a few doors. The local hairdressers, barber shops or laundromats are always full of people who aren't shy about voicing opinions.

Ask them anything you want to. Get the overall "feel" or im-

pression of the neighborhood from the owner's viewpoint. Are
they bullish on the area and its present and future? Are they
proud of their neighborhood? Are they involved in the Little
League? The Lions Club? Church groups? Are they investing
their time and energy in the area? Are the owners upwardly
mobile people, or is the area somewhat staid? What do people
your age do for entertainment? What does the community offer
to keep the kids busy and off the streets?

Questions like these are fair game, and should elicit some sur-
prising responses. You don't have to worry about being snubbed,
because people love to talk about themselves and their activities
and investment in their home. Have fun and be yourself!

GET HELP FROM BUSINESS EXPERTS

The business experts can be located in the phone book. Talk
to the bankers, home-lending institutions, mortgage companies,
insurance people, builders, and retailers. Simply tell them you
were thinking about buying a home in the area, and you would
appreciate their opinion and any statistics they could offer you.
Ask specifically about property values and the traditional appreciation rate of the area's homes. Lenders can also tell you if there
is a strong demand for homes in the area, as evidenced by quick
sales. What about the businesses in the area? Are they stable
concerns with an eye toward the future? Remember, a personal
visit will be more fruitful, and who knows, you may make a new
friend or meet a lender who can help you later!

WHERE TO GET ECONOMIC DATA

Economic data is collected by various branches of local government. Wander around city hall and someone will help you
find the proper office for planning, zoning, growth plans, or
what-have-you. Talk to someone in a position to help you focus
on the future growth plans and zoning scheme. Non-government
groups may also be of help, especially the Chamber of Commerce.

The Board of Education should also be on your list of places to
visit. It has all sorts of statistics, especially on children (potential
playmates for yours).

THE USE OF REAL ESTATE SALESPEOPLE

Professional real estate salespeople can provide a wealth of information and can assist you in selecting the right neighborhood. Should you seek their services or not? It is appropriate at this juncture to summarize a few cogent aspects of the relationship of salespeople with the people they deal with.

A "listing agreement" is the contract of employment between the owner (seller) of a home and the broker (or most often the broker's agent, the salesperson). The owner agrees to pay a certain commission to the broker if the home is sold for a specified price. Commissions vary from area to area, but fees in the 5-percent-to-7-percent range are common.

But you're not the seller—you're the buyer! When a salesperson shows you homes, there is *no* employment contract between you and him or her. The professional is trying to sell the home for his client, the seller. What this means to you, the buyer, is that you pay *zero* commission to the salesperson. The seller pays the entire commission, absent any agreement to the contrary. To check up on this custom in your own, ask any broker. So, since the services of a pro are free to the buyer, should you use one?

WHAT THE PROS CAN DO FOR YOU

A pro can show you which homes have sold in the last year and tell you the sales prices. By checking sales over the last few years, a pro can give you an idea of the average appreciation for homes in the neighborhood. (Lending institutions can give you this information also.) It is wise to ask that information given by pros be written down. That way you can protect yourself should you rely upon the misrepresentations of a fraudulent or poor professional.

Communication is the key toward a good working relationship with real estate salespeople. Tell them what you want done, and ask for their opinion and help. Choose a salesperson or broker as carefully as you would any other professional. If you don't know a pro, ask your friends or relatives or neighbors to recommend a few. Or you can ask your lender or lawyer to give you the names of several reputable firms. If in doubt, phone three or four different people from different firms, and interview them. Pick the one you think can do the most for you!

The following checklist is designed to help you evaluate neighborhoods, utilizing key criteria.

Checklist for Evaluating Neighborhoods

(1) Market Prices

Are the homes in the neighborhood appreciating at a rate above or equal to the town's average rate of increase?

(2) Existing Homes

Are the homes basically homogeneous in price, or is there a wide range in prices? (In bigger towns, a wide variety can slow appreciation for the higher-priced homes.)

Are the homes consistent in style(s)?

Do most of the residents own their own homes?

Do the homes appear to be well cared for (painted, repaired, etc.)?

Are the lawns and grounds well kept?

Is there enough off-street parking for residents' cars?

(3) New Construction

Are the vacant lots in the neighborhood in demand for new home building?

Are the new homes being constructed priced in line with the existing homes? (If higher, that's a good sign.)

If the whole subdivision is new, consider this: Are the builders/developers reputable; and how have their past ventures fared? Have they appreciated well?

(4) Schools

Can the kids walk to school?

If not, is a bus provided? Any cost for this?

Is the faculty well qualified?

Are sufficient extracurricular activities offered?

Schools (cont.)

Do the students fare well on standard exams (like the SAT) ?

Do the parents have the desired voice in school affairs?

Are the schools free from violence?

(5) Transportation

Are the streets and highways adequate to handle traffic flow? Remember, *you* have to drive home after work!

Is public transportation available, if needed?

Is there adequate parking for business needs?

(6) Shopping and Business Sections

Is there a sufficient range of goods and services available?

Are new enterprises attracted to the area?

Are older businesses growing and staying in the area?

Do the residents patronize their neighborhood stores?

Are prices and quality competitive?

Is there sufficient capital investment to suggest that proprietors plan to be there a long time?

(7) Public Facilities

Is there adequate recreational space?

Is there a park with activities for the kids?

Is there a library nearby?

(8) Safety

Do the residents feel safe on their streets?

Is there good lighting for public areas?

Is there sufficient police protection?

Is the crime rate acceptable, when compared to other areas?

Safety (cont.)

Is there a fire station reasonably close?

Is there a hospital nearby or easy to reach?

(9) Adjacent Neighborhoods

Are they similar in character and price range when compared to your neighborhood?

Are the surrounding areas safe to travel through?

Are property values holding up well?

Are the fringe areas where neighborhoods meet desirable to buyers, or is the lower income area growing?

(10) Special Considerations

This is a do-it-yourself section. Here, *you* must jot down on a piece of paper any specific criteria that you *must* have in the neighborhood you wish to live in. For example: it must be in the XYZ school district; it must be close to the Aquinas Church; it must have a Little League program for Junior; it must be close to your parents' home, etc.

8
Selecting Your Home

Now that you have selected one or several desirable neighborhoods that are within your price range, the next step is really the fun step! You search for that special house that will become your home.

USING PROFESSIONAL HELP

A good real estate salesperson can save you hours of time and some of your sanity. Merely give the pro your criteria, such as: neighborhood, price range, number of bedrooms, and any features that you desire (such as fireplaces, two bathrooms, two-car garage, patio, central air, or whatever you wish). Let the pros do all the research and legwork. As mentioned before, the seller pays the commission. The pro's services are free to the buyer.

SEARCHING ON YOUR OWN

What if the very thought of salespeople conjures up bad vibes and visions of "being pressured"? Or what if you think it would be more fun to do it yourself! Where do you begin?

There are two basic search procedures. First, check the newspaper for real estate ads. Grab a felt-tipped pen and circle the homes that are in your neighborhood and range. If no area is mentioned, perhaps the phone number will give you a clue. Use the telephone to do your legwork. Call to find out if the home has most of the things you desire. If your interest is piqued, make an appointment to see the home.

The second method is to drive through the neighborhood. Take a small notebook with you so you can jot down addresses and phone numbers. Later, you can phone to ask whether the houses meet your basic requirements. If so, make an appointment.

OPEN HOUSES

Many people "drive around neighborhoods" on Sunday after-noons. You know the scene—kids who want to go to the bathroom or visit Ronald McDonald, or mothers-in-law who are experts because they own their home already. There is usually someone in the car who remarks, "Real estate is so high these days!"

Oftentimes an "open house" is held on Sundays, to catch some of this cruising traffic. An open house allows potential buyers to view the home on the spur of the moment, without an ap-pointment.

Take heed of the following practical pointers. If an owner holds an open house, he does so for one reason—he wants to sell the place. However, real estate salesmen hold open houses for several reasons: 1) to give the owner a little action, and sell the house if possible; 2) to gain new buyers who may not like this home, but can be talked into visiting other homes with the pro; and 3) to gain new sellers, such as interested neighbors who are thinking of selling and want to get an idea about price ranges in the neighborhood. So if you don't wish to have salespeople bug you about other properties that are for sale in the area, make it clear to them.

THE SELLER'S MOTIVE

You can often find out why the owner is selling his home. Was he transferred? Is this home too small for the family? Too big? Have they purchased another home already? If the owner has a strong motive to sell, perhaps a price lower than the "asking price" will be accepted. Motive may be discovered through con-versation with the owner or members of the family. Smart sales-people rarely tip their owner's hand.

FOR-SALE-BY-OWNER . . . A BARGAIN?

Are for-sale-by-owners better buys than those offered by real estate brokers? Can a buyer save the usual 6 percent or 7 percent commission that a seller pays the broker? Usually, no! After all, why should a seller do all the work and pay all the advertising expenses that a broker usually does, and then give the commission away to the buyer in the form of a 6 percent or 7 percent price reduction? Using a broker, the owner loses the commission. Selling at a reduced price, the owner also loses his time and effort. That is why less than 5 percent of all homes are sold by owners!

Once in a blue moon owners may lack the knowledge to price their home properly. Perhaps you could make a nice buy at below market value in such a situation. Don't hold your breath, though.

VIEWING THE HOME

The first time you go through a home, just enjoy it! Do the floor plan, style, and price range meet with your approval? Are the features and benefits pleasing? Can you imagine yourself living in this home?

If all the decision-makers in your family like the home, you will want to gather more information. I recommend that you ask the owner's permission to return later, or the next day, to do some inspecting in your old clothes. Pick a time when there are still a few hours of daylight present, and a time when the owner can be present to answer questions.

You don't have to be an expert to make the simple inspections that are listed for you in the following checklist. The purpose of your inspection is to spot any potential big repairs, big headaches, and big expenses. If serious doubts arise, it may be worth your while to hire an expert to examine the house or problem area.

For example, I live most of the year in the Tulsa area, and utilize the services of EMP, Inc., which specializes in the electrical, mechanical, plumbing, and structural analysis of a home for the buyer. Similar services may be available in your area, or you might try phoning the local building inspector for leads. (Oftentimes they know some moonlighters.)

Remember, all older homes have some wear and tear. That is why they are cheaper than similar new homes. Realize this, but avoid major problems. Also realize that you can specifically state in your offer to purchase that the owner repair this or that problem. Your attorney can draw this up to your specifications.

Use the following checklist to aid in your inspection.

Inspection Checklist

(1) Roof

Crawl up into the attic. Look at the wood on the roof. Is there any sign of leakage?

Is there any rotten wood? Check the beams, especially in the corners. You can test the wood with an icepick or screwdriver. Poke it!

Is the insulation adequate for your area's weather?

Look at the wiring up there, if there is any. Are the wires worn or frazzled?

How old is the exterior roof? (Ask the owner.)

Look at the roof yourself. Is the roof in good shape, or will you have to reshingle it or put composition tar sheets on it soon?

Has the roof ever leaked to the owner's knowledge?

Are the gutters in good repair?

Do the gutters drain properly? If need be, stick a hose up there and find out. This also helps spot leaky joints.

Is the wood around the gutters or edge of the roof free of rot and decay?

Are the eaves under the roof free of rot and decay?

(2) Floors

Are the floors fairly level? Or have they settled too much in spots, suggesting possible structural weaknesses? A simple test is rolling a marble on the floor and watching it.

Crawl under the house, if possible. It's messy, but important. Is there any rotten wood? Poke around with your ice pick or screwdriver.

Are the support beams in good shape? Check particularly where they rest on the foundation.

Floors (cont.)

Look for the plumbing pipes. Are there any signs of leakage or damage? Look carefully at any wood around the pipes, being sure it isn't rotten.

Go inside and check the basement floor, if there is one. Is there any sign of flooding stains there or on the walls? Any abnormal cracks on walls or floor? Ask the owner about flooding in the past.

If you have doubts, talk to a few neighbors. Ask them if they ever had water in their basements. Sometimes people lie . . .

(3) Plumbing

Go into the bathroom(s). Do the taps run freely and with clean water?

Is there enough pressure? Turn the taps up full blast! Then flush the toilet.

Do the faucets drip? Do telltale stains in the sink suggest drips or leaks?

Look at the pipes and floor under the sink or basin area. Any problem signs?

Is the toilet bowl well secured to the floor? Sit on it! Any rocking suggests problems underneath.

Does the toilet flush and refill properly? Take the top off and observe the parts at work.

Run the shower or bath. Any drips or leaks?

Is there sufficient water pressure?

Check the plumbing in the kitchen and utility room. Whenever possible, poke around under the sinks and look for any problem signs.

(4) Heating and Cooling

Any past repairs or problems? (Ask the owner.)

Call the company that serviced the system if you desire more information.

(5) Water Heaters

Is the capacity enough for your needs? Usually a thirty-gallon tank will do the job for a family of four. Larger families may require up to fifty-gallon tanks.

Is it properly vented?

Is the tank rusting out?

Are the controls working properly?

Are there any signs of leakage on the floor?

(6) Exterior

Are there signs of mortar deterioration in the brick walls?

Are the steps in good condition?

Is the wood in good shape, particularly around the windows, doors, and porch?

Is the cement in walks and driveways in good shape?

Can you safely negotiate the driveway in all types of weather?

Does the driveway allow clear vision of street traffic?

Is there a vertical crack evident at the ground level of the foundation, suggesting structural problems?

(7) Interior

Did you measure the entire house and sketch a rough floor plan? Is there enough space for your furniture and other belongings?

Are the stairs easily negotiated by family members?

Is storage space adequate?

Interior (cont.)

> Did you check insulation and R-values? Ask to see relevant utility bills.

(8) Environmental

> Does the property drain adequately and the runoff flow away from the foundation? Does runoff remain in puddles on patio or driveway?
>
> How does your floor plan relate to sunlight? As a general rule, the rooms you use the most in the daytime should face south.
>
> Are there any noises that distract you from enjoying the home, such as factories, trains, airplanes, or cars? A check at various times of the day is advisable.

(9) Landscape

> Are there any rotten trees that can be expensive to remove?
>
> Does the lawn require a lot of time or money to maintain? How about the shrubs?
>
> Could tree roots clog up the plumbing? Ask the owner if this has been a past problem.

(10) Electrical

> When was the house last rewired?
>
> Are there adequate outlets? Is a 220 line needed for air-conditioning units, utilities, appliances, etc.?

(11) Windows and Doors

> Do they open with ease?
>
> Are they hung properly?
>
> Are the locks in working order and adequate for your security?

(12) Before Signing

After you have decided to make an offer to purchase a home, call your attorney before you sign anything. Don't try to be a do-it-yourself lawyer. If you're investing thousands in a home, why not protect yourself by spending a hundred or two?

Therefore, last but not least, is our final checklist item: Call your lawyer *before* signing offer to purchase!

9

Conventional Loans

As the word suggests, "conventional" loans are normal, everyday home loans. A conventional loan is not a government-insured loan (FHA), nor a government-guaranteed loan (VA).

For conventional loans, the lender's only security is the property; therefore, the lender will usually require a 20 percent or 25 percent down payment. This sizeable initial investment by the buyer minimizes the risk for lenders.

INSURED CONVENTIONAL LOANS

There is a type of conventional loan that features a lower down payment, called the *insured* conventional loan. The property and the buyer must both meet the private insurer's qualifications. This private insurer guarantees the lender that the top 20 percent of the loan will be repaid, in the event of a default by the borrower. The private insurer sells the borrower Private Mortgage Insurance, known as PMI. The usual charge for this PMI is ¼ percent tacked on to the interest rate. The borrower can also expect to pay a one-time fee of ½ percent at closing to the private concern.

PMI makes everyone happy! The lending institution is happy because the private insurer has guaranteed the top 20 percent, which is the risky part of the loan. The bottom, or remaining 80 percent of the loan is usually safely secured by the property itself. The buyer is happy, because his initial costs are reduced! Instead of a 20 percent down payment, the buyer may only need 10 percent, for example. (A 20 percent down payment on a $40,000 home is $8,000. But a 10 percent down payment is only $4,000! That saves the buyer $4,000 in cash that would be due at closing.) And of course the private insurer is happy, too! He's making money by charging ¼ percent.

You can get up to a 95 percent insured conventional loan, if you and the property qualify. Usually the home must be no more than twelve to fifteen years old. The homes are usually priced in the median or slightly lower price ranges. Private insurers have their own rules that vary. When you visit lenders, ask about the availability of these programs in your area, and what guidelines you must meet to qualify for PMI.

Savings and loan associations, banks, and life insurance companies are the major sources of conventional loans.

AN EXAMPLE

Let's work through a complete example of conventional financing. Assume you want to purchase a $40,000 home. You plan to get a 90 percent conventional loan at 11 percent for thirty years (10¾ + ¼ PMI). What will your approximate cost be? Just how much cash will you need to have at closing?

DOWN PAYMENT

The sales price of the home is $40,000. Since the loan is a 90 percent loan, the down payment is 10 percent of the purchase price. The loan amount is the purchase price ($40,000), minus the down payment ($4,000), or $36,000. .

LOAN ORIGINATION FEES

Lenders charge the borrowers a loan fee—that is, to say it another way, for the privilege of borrowing the lender's money, you will pay a one-time-only fee, due at closing. This fee is sometimes expressed in "points." One point equals 1 percent. One-half point equals ½ of 1 percent, and so on.

To calculate your loan origination fee, multiply the loan amount ($36,000) times the points. For example, suppose your lender charges 1 percent. The loan origination fee is $36,000 ×

.01, equalling a $360 fee. (Remember to express the percentages in decimal form!)

CLOSING COSTS

Individual lenders set different costs for the following items: appraisal of the property, credit check, survey of the property, inspection fee, photograph of property, amortization schedule, attorney's opinion for the lender, recording and abstract costs, title insurance, escrow fees, and perhaps some other miscellaneous costs. To get an approximate idea of the cost of these services, phone your lender.

ESCROW ITEMS OR PREPAIDS

These costs are paid by the buyer before the closing date. Prepaids are also referred to as "escrows," because they are held in trust by a loan officer or escrow agent.

INSURANCE ESCROWS

Because the lender has a very big stake in your purchase, he wants to be sure that the home is properly insured at all times. What good would the collateral (your home) be if it was destroyed by fire or damaged? Therefore, do not forget or neglect to properly insure your home.

A thirteen-month escrow deposit for insurance is normally required by the lending institutions. To arrive at an exact figure, call your agent for insurance needs and ask for a quote on your $40,000 home. For purposes of a very rough yardstick, you can use this formula to determine your monthly insurance costs:

$$1 \text{ month's insurance} = \frac{\text{value of home}}{\$2,000} + \$3$$

Using our $40,000 home example, the monthly insurance escrow would be equal to: $40,000 divided by $2,000; or $20 + $3 = $23. The total escrow for insurance requires thirteen months of reserve funds. Therefore, $23 times 13 = $299 for insurance escrow.

TAX ESCROW

The lender also wants to make sure that there is not a tax lien on his collateral (your home), so he requires a three-month tax escrow amount. Taxes vary widely in different areas. To get an estimate of taxes for the price range you are interested in, ask a lender. If you have a specific home already picked out, ask the owner what his taxes are, or call the county assessor's office. Divide the yearly taxes by four, to get the three-month escrow figure. Assume the taxes on your $40,000 home are $400 per year. The escrow would be $400 divided by four, or $100.

PREPAID INTEREST

Prepaid interest is the interest accumulated from the closing date until the end of the particular month in which the closing took place. For example, let us say your loan closed on June 15th. Your prepaid interest would be fifteen days' worth, to cover the use of the lender's money for the last fifteen days of June. Your first monthly payment is then due August 1st. (The first day of the month is usually the agreed-upon date.) So your first payment is made *after* the lender's money has been used. The interest prepayment is paid *before* the money is used, in order to adjust the payments to the day chosen for monthly payments to be made.

The prepaid interest amount is one month at the maximum. It is best to compute a full thirty days' interest, to avoid any surprises at closing. To compute this amount, use this formula: 1) Loan amount × interest rate = one year's interest; then, 2) One year's interest divided by twelve months = one month's interest.

So, for our $40,000 home with a loan amount of $36,000, we compute the prepaid interest as follows: (1) $36,000 × .11 = $3,960; (2) $3,960 divided by 12 = $330 (1 month's interest).

ATTORNEYS' FEES

Your attorney serves you all through the home-buying process, but he really takes over when the negotiations are firmed into a contract. Before the closing date, your attorney will examine your title, and clear up any problems. He will also guide matters to a head, with the closing being the culmination of his efforts. At the closing (and before), you will be signing all sorts of affidavits, forms, and paper with legal mumbo-jumbo on it. You will be advised what you are signing and why. To get an idea of what this will cost you, phone your attorney or local bar association.

Some attorneys charge a flat fee; others charge a percentage of the purchase price (in the range of ½ to 1 percent). So, for our $40,000-home example, plan on 1 percent or $400 maximum to be budgeted for lawyers' fees.

WORKSHEETS

The following worksheet summarizes typical costs you will have to meet for conventional loans using our $40,000 home as an example.

Worksheet for Conventional Loans

Down Payment = Sales price of home *minus* loan amount.

Loan Origination Fee = Loan amount *times* "points" (in decimal form). (Remember: 1 point = 1% = .01).

Prepaids or Escrows
(1) Insurance =
> Phone your insurance agent
> or
> a) $\dfrac{\text{sales price}}{\$2,000} + \$3.00 = 1$ month's insurance;
> then, b) 1 month's insurance *times* 13 months = escrow amount.

(2) Tax = Phone: owner, broker, or county assessor's office; then *divide* yearly taxes by 4 to get 3 month figure. (Some lenders might require 6–12 months. Ask them.)

(3) Interest = a) 1 year's interest = loan amount *times* interest rate; then b) 1 year's interest *divided by* 12 = 1 month's interest (1 month is the maximum charge).

Closing Costs = Phone your lender. Each lender sets his own.

Attorney's Fee = Phone your lawyer or local Bar Association. Expect fee of ½ to 1 percent of purchase price. Some lawyers charge flat fee.

Worksheet

Address: _____   Type of Loan: _____

Price: _____   Interest rate: _____

Down Payment: _____

Loan Origination Fee: _____

Insurance Prepaids: _____

Tax Prepaids: _____

Interest Prepaids: _____

Closing Costs: _____

Attorney's Fee: _____

Total Costs Due
At Closing   _____

CONVENTIONAL LOANS AND FLEXIBLE PAYMENT PLANS

Realizing that many people want homes, but have a little trouble financing them, lenders have designed flexible monthly payment plans. The salient feature of this type of conventional loan is that for the first few years a buyer's monthly payments are reduced, as the borrower pays interest and escrows only. There is no payment to reduce the principal loan amount, until after a number of years. The number of years varies with each specific lender's programs, but five years is a common number.

AN EXAMPLE

Suppose a savings and loan association offers the following program: For the first five years the borrower pays only interest and escrows. After five years, the principal is included in the monthly payments, and the loan balance is amortized over the remaining twenty-five years of the loan term.

You want to buy a $25,000 home. How would this flexible program work for you? Assume that your monthly escrows total $62.00. The lender will give you a 90 percent insured conventional loan, at 9 percent (PMI included). Your loan amount will be $22,500.

To determine your monthly payments, first compute one month's interest. Use this formula:

(1) Loan amount × interest rate (decimal form) = 1 year's interest;

(2) One year's interest *divided by* 12 = 1 month's interest.

Now that we know what one month's interest is, we make the following final computation:

(3) One month's interest + monthly escrows = monthly payments.

Therefore, in our example:

(1) $22,500 × .09 = $2,025 (1 year's interest);

(2) $2,025 ÷ 12 = $168.75;

(3) $168.75 + $62 (escrows) = $230.75 monthly payments.

To make $230.75 monthly payments under the flexible program, your gross income should be $920 a month or more, in order to qualify for the $22,500 loan.

For the first five years, you will make monthly payments of $230.75. After five years, you will begin to make payments that include amounts to reduce your principal. In effect, at the end of the fifth year your loan amount is still $22,500; but now you must pay it off in twenty-five years. Your monthly payments at the start of the sixth year would be about $255.

If you simply wanted a regular thirty-year loan at 9 percent for $22,500, your monthly payments would have been $243, and you would need a monthly income of $972 to qualify.

THE ADVANTAGES OF THIS PROGRAM

The main advantage is that you need a smaller monthly income to qualify for the desired loan amount. (You need $920 in our example.) Five years from now, you will need a gross monthly income of $1,004 or greater, in order to make those $255 payments. The lender is supposing that your salary will rise less than $100 a month ($84, to be exact!) over the next five years. That's less than a 10 percent raise, spread over five years. That's a pretty safe assumption, especially for young college graduates or professional people on the way up.

Should it alarm you that after five years of payments, you still owe the exact same figure ($22,500) that you borrowed? Absolutely not! Suppose home values rise at a 10 percent rate in your neighborhood. After five years, your home is worth about $40,000. You still owe $22,500, leaving you an equity of $17,500.

The flexible programs, therefore, increase your buying power by reducing front-end payments, and allowing you to qualify for a more expensive home. To find out if the lenders in your area have such programs, give them a call.

RENEGOTIATED RATE LOANS

The Federal Home Loan Bank Board has proposed a "renegotiated rate mortgage" that could become the major vehicle for home financing in periods of economic uncertainty.

How would this proposed loan work?

Federally chartered savings and loans could issue up to thirty-year-mortgaged loans, but the interest rate would *not* be fixed for the life of the loan. The interest rate would be renegotiated every three to five years. The lender could raise the interest rate by no more than ½ of 1 percent a year, and no greater than a total of 5 percent over the life of the loan (usually thirty years).

On the flip side of the coin, the buyer would benefit from a fall in prevailing interest rates, because the lender must decrease the rate by mandate. There would also be no prepayment penalty after the first renewal, should the buyer wish to refinance or pay off the loan.

Here's an example of how this new loan might be used by you:

Suppose you buy a home on January 1, 1986. You get a thirty-year mortgage, at say 13 percent, to be renegotiated every three years. By 1989, prevailing interest rates may be back to 9 percent. At the renegotiation date, the lender must offer you this lower rate for three more years.

To find out more about this program, call your savings and loan and ask if (or when) they will offer a renegotiated rate loan, or as some people refer to it, "the Canadian Rollover Mortgage." Because this program is more acceptable to lenders than the variable rate mortgage, it should help make money for home loans more available.

SPECIAL LOW-INTEREST LOANS

Over the last few years, many cities and counties have sponsored low-interest rate, home loan programs. Where does the money come from? It is raised by the sale of tax-exempt revenue bonds. Let's suppose that the interest rate is 8½ percent, compared to the 15 percent rate prevailing in the market. This tax-free status induces investors to buy the bonds, buyers get cheap rates, and politicians look like heroes.

How do you get your hands on this cheap money? Phone or visit the Housing Authority in your area and ask if they have such a program, or are planning one. Now, let me scare you— the demand for these loans is incredible! You have to be persistent and well-informed. Stay in touch constantly with the program's director.

Is it worth your effort? Consider this: A $50,000 loan for thirty years at 15 percent means $632 in monthly payments on principal and interest. But at say 8½ percent, your monthly payments would be $384. Does saving $248 a month excite you?

SHARED APPRECIATION MORTGAGES

Private lenders have received phenomenal response to new programs that offer home buyers a significantly reduced interest rate in return for a share in the future appreciation of the home.

Suppose you make $22,000 a year, and have $10,000 to put down on a $60,000 home. Suppose current interest rates are 15 percent. Monthly payments on a $50,000 loan for thirty years at 15 percent would be $632. You would need a gross income of $2,528 a month (or $30,336 a year) to qualify for such a loan. Since you only make $22,000 a year, you can't qualify—no home!

What if a lender were to give you a 10 percent interest rate (a full third less than the prevailing 15 percent rate) if you in turn promise the lender one-third of the future appreciation of the home! Sound good? Let's check the arithmetic. At 10 percent, a $50,000 loan requires monthly payments of $439, and a monthly gross income of $1,756 (or $21,072 a year) to qualify. So, your monthly payments would be almost $200 lower, and you could qualify with $9,000 less in salary!

Is the trade off worth it? That's your decision. Considering our above example, I'd say it's better to have two-thirds of *something* than all of *nothing!*

Most lending activity of this kind has occurred recently in Florida, California, and New York. The Federal Home Loan Bank Board has proposed regulations to allow savings and loans all over America to offer shared appreciation mortgages. These regulations would require the savings and loan association to refinance the loan after ten years, if you have not sold the house by then. The lender's share of the appreciation would be included in this refinancing.

Call your local savings and loan association to find out if and when they plan to offer SAM to you.

10
FHA Loans

The role of the FHA is one of the most misunderstood concepts among non-homeowners. Since 1971, the Federal Housing Administration (FHA) has been part of the Department of Housing and Urban Development (HUD).

To facilitate wider home ownership, FHA *insures* loans made by approved lenders to qualified buyers of qualified properties. FHA itself is not in the lending business! The borrower is charged ½ percent of the loan amount to pay these insurance premiums. These premiums are included in the borrower's monthly payments to the lender.

TODAY'S PROGRAMS

FHA has a variety of programs, but we are concerned only with residential home buying. In this chapter we will analyze the 203B program, the 221D-2 program, and highlight several other programs.

BACKGROUND AND IMPACT ON LENDERS

First of all, let's get a historical perspective of the FHA. FHA was born in 1934, in depression days. Easy money in the 1920s contributed significantly to our nation's economic woes. One could not accuse home mortgage lenders of making money easily available! Typical home loans required 50 percent down payments, and were only three to five years in length. The loans were not amortized: that is, periodic payments did not include payments to reduce the principal (loan amount).

The FHA's stated purpose was to improve housing standards

and create a sound mortgage market. Its real purpose was basically twofold. First, FHA was formed to stimulate the construction industry, and get the suppliers, laborers, and craftsmen back to work. FHA's second purpose was to shift the risk of mortgage defaults from private lenders to the government, through FHA's insuring of the loans.

Prior to the FHA's creation, lenders placed their emphasis on the *property* as security, and the 50 percent down payments gave the lender a good cushion, should the borrower default.

The impact of the FHA was to shift this emphasis on property as the security for the loan to the individual's earning power as the security for the loan. With this shift in emphasis grew the need for refined appraisal methods, and more sophisticated and detailed credit checks.

FHA's biggest influence on lenders was to introduce the self-amortizing mortgage with a long life of fifteen, twenty, and later thirty years. Gradually, private lenders had to adopt these practices to remain competitive.

Now, let's get back to the present and explain how the three most widely used FHA programs operate.

FHA 203B PROGRAM

About 70 percent of all the FHA insured loans that have been made utilize this type of financing program. The program is available for use by single and married people. Contrary to some notions, it is *not* restricted for use by low-income groups!

The maximum insured loan for a single-family dwelling is $82,500 under 203B, as of late 1985. This figure is periodically revised.

DOWN PAYMENT NEEDED

The required down payment fluctuates with the loan amount you desire. If the appraised value of the home is below $50,000, the down payment is 3 percent of the appraised value. If the appraised value is above $50,000, then the down payment is 3 percent of the first $25,000 in appraised value, plus 5 percent of the amount above $25,000. For example, let's suppose you want to buy a $70,000 home. To determine the loan amount and down payment, calculate in this manner:

(1) List the appraised value of the home (not the asking or sales price, but the appraised value made by the FHA).

$70,000 (1)

(2) Add the FHA scheduled closing costs to the appraised value. (The schedule is reproduced on page 71.)

$$\begin{aligned} \$70,000 \\ + \ \$ \ 1,400 \\ \hline \$71,400 \ \ (2) \end{aligned}$$

(3) 97% of $25,000 = $24,250
95% of $46,400 = $44,080
Add these figures to get loan amount.

$$\begin{aligned} \$24,250 \\ + \ \$44,080 \\ \hline \$68,330 \ \ (3) \end{aligned}$$

(4) Round (3) down to nearest multiple of $50.

$68,300 (4)

(5) Appraised value *minus* loan amount (4) equals the down payment.

$$\begin{aligned} \$70,000 \\ - \ \$68,300 \\ \hline \$ \ 1,700 \ \ (5) \end{aligned}$$

Suppose you wanted to buy a home appraised at $44,000. How would you compute the loan amount and down payment?

(1) Appraised value. $44,000

(2) Add FHA scheduled closing costs.

$$\begin{aligned} \$44,000 \\ + \ \ \ \ 850 \\ \hline \$44,850 \ \ (2) \end{aligned}$$

(3) 97% of $25,000 = $24,250
90% of $10,000 = $9,000
80% of $9,000 + $850 (closing costs) = $8,050

Add these figures to get loan amount.

$$\begin{aligned} \$24,250 \\ + \ 9,000 \\ + \ 8,050 \\ \hline \$41,300 \ \ (3) \end{aligned}$$

(4) Round (3) down to nearest multiple of $50. (Note: it is already in proper form.

$41,300 (4)

(5) Appraised value *minus* loan amount (4) equals the down payment.

$$\begin{aligned} \$44,000 \\ - \ \ 41,300 \\ \hline \$ \ 2,700 = \text{down payment} \end{aligned}$$

FHA CLOSING COSTS

The closing costs are determined by the FHA. FHA sets these fees, and publishes them in a schedule. FHA does this to prevent lenders from padding the costs with extras or additional fees for the *buyer*.

As for conventional loans, the items covered by this scheduled fee include: appraisal, credit check, survey, inspection fee, photograph of property, amortization schedule, recording and abstract fees, attorney's opinion for the lender, and a loan origination fee charged to the buyer.

For your own reference, the schedule of FHA closing costs is reproduced on page 71.

To be sure of the current FHA schedule, phone your local FHA-HUD office. You could also call a savings and loan association or mortgage company. Banks generally do not make FHA loans.

OTHER COSTS

You must also be prepared to pay your attorney's fees, and your tax escrows, insurance escrows, and prepaid interest at closing. These costs are detailed, explained, and calculated in the chapter on conventional loans. They are computed in the same manner as therein described.

FHA 203B WORKSHEETS

The following worksheets may be used by the reader to estimate the total costs the buyer will initially need. (Costs referred to are "financial costs." Other initial costs are what I term "moving costs," such as utility deposits, paying for a moving van or U-Haul, etc.)

Worksheet for FHA 203B Loans

Buyer's Closing Costs = See the FHA schedule (in this chapter).

Loan Amount = If loan is below $50,000:
97% of loan amount _____(a)
OR: If loan is above $50,000:
97% of first $25,000 _____(b)
plus: 95% of remaining amount _____ (c)
Total either (a) *OR* (b) + (c) ——————(d)
(e) If appraised value of home is less than $50,000, add to (d) 97% of closing costs. If appraised value of home is above $50,000, add to (d) 95% of closing costs.

(d) _____ + (e) _____ = total loan amount.

Down Payment = Sales Price of Home *minus* Loan Amount.

Prepaids or Escrows

(1) Insurance = Phone your insurance agent; or
a) $\frac{\text{sales price} + \$3.00}{\$2,000}$ = 1 month's insurance;
then, b) 1 month's insurance *times* 13 months = escrow amount.

(2) Tax = Phone: owner, broker, or county assessor's office, then: *divide* yearly taxes by 4 to get 3 month figure. (Some lenders may require more than 3 months' escrow.)

(3) Interest = a) 1 year's interest = loan amount *times* interest rate; then b) 1 year's interest *divided by* 12 = 1 month's interest.

Attorney's Fee = Phone your lawyer or local Bar Association. Fee range: ½% to 1% of purchase price, or flat fee.

Worksheet

Address: _____   Type of Loan: _____

Price: _____   Interest Rate: _____

Buyer's Closing Costs: _____

Loan Amount: _____

Down Payment: _____

Insurance Prepaids: _____

Tax Prepaids: _____

Interest Prepaids: _____

Attorney's Fee: _____

            Total Costs Due
            At Closing   _____

FHA-REQUIRED REPAIRS

Another major stumbling block to FHA arrangements is the cost of required repairs. Before the loan is finalized, an FHA inspector visits the house and appraises its condition. A list of things that need repairs or improvements is made. FHA standards are the measuring stick. The requirements must be met in order for the loan to be approved.

Who pays for these requirements? The basic answer is that you must look to the provisions of your contract for sale. Most contracts state a maximum dollar amount that both the buyer and seller are willing to pay.

What happens when the requirements will cost more than the contracting parties agreed to be responsible for? If this happened, either party could cancel the entire deal, or both parties could arrive at a new supplementary agreement to the contract, fixing responsibility for these costs in a new manner.

Contracts sometimes are written in a manner providing for low maximum amounts for the parties to pay for requirements. Why? First, it gives either party an out, if they want it. Second, some real estate salespeople do not want to argue with the parties until a later date. At this later date, both parties have psychologically committed themselves to the sale and purchase of "their home." They'll grumble, but almost always go through with the deal.

To beat this mind-game, a seller may have an FHA appraisal done ahead of time, before he puts his home on the market. This must be done through a lender, who will then tell the seller that if a qualified buyer is found in sixty or ninety days, and the requirements are met, the lender will finance the deal based on the appraised value.

FHA ESTIMATES

Besides the list of requirements, the FHA also provides an estimate of the costs you can expect to encounter in meeting the requirements.

Do *not* rely on this estimate! It is almost always too low!

The FHA inspector spends only a brief time looking over your selected home. The inspection is not meant to be a complete checkup. For example, the inspectors don't usually crawl under the home or up in the attic. Suppose they find some rotten wood under the eaves of the roof or around the gutters. The eye cannot tell how extensive the rot is, for you would probably have to rip up the shingles to see how bad things really are. This example shows you why you cannot rely on estimates.

Here's another tip for you as a buyer: the seller can allow the buyer a credit for doing all or any portion of the required repairs. This would save the buyer some initial costs. This credit amount cannot exceed the FHA's estimates, however.

BORROWING THE DOWN PAYMENT

The FHA does not allow the buyer to borrow the down payment, for two basic reasons. First, it reduces the owner (buyer's) psychological stake in the home-buying venture; and secondly, private mortgage lenders regard this as a poor financing device. If you plan to borrow some money, do it *before* you sign a contract to buy a house. Put the loan in your bank account.

KNOW YOUR BARGAINING POSITION

Homes in the under $60,000 range are the ones that are most likely to secure an FHA loan, since the buyers in that price range are less likely to have the liquidity to pay higher down payments and fees. Ask a lender or broker in your area what percentage of the homes in the range you can afford sell with FHA financing. This will give you a clearer picture as to the seller's expectations.

With all these problems, why does a seller agree to FHA financing? Because it is the best offer he thinks he can get!

FHA 221D-2 PROGRAM

The other most commonly used FHA program is the 221D-2. It was designed in 1954 to insure mortgages for rehabilitating homes and replacing slums with new housing for displaced people. However, in 1961 the program was expanded to include any family with a low or moderate income. Today, it is for low or moderate income *families only*.

As of late 1985, the maximum loan was $38,000 for a three-bed-room house, and $44,000 for a four-bedroom house with five or more family members living in it. These figures are revised from time to time, as soaring real estate values make adjustments necessary. If in doubt, call the FHA or a lender.

ADVANTAGES OF PROGRAM

The 221D-2 program is frequently referred to as the "no down payment" program, which aptly describes its effect and major advantage.

Note that the seller is allowed to pay the buyer's closing costs, but the buyer must pay his own escrows or prepaids. If the seller does pay the buyer's closing costs, the FHA and lenders will normally require that the buyer have some financial stake in the home. As a rule of thumb, the prepaids plus closing costs are considered a sufficient stake for the buyer's initial investment. The potential problem areas referred to in the section about the 203B program are also applicable here.

LOAN AMOUNTS

To determine the loan amount, take the value of the home *plus closing costs,* and find 97 percent of this sum. Then add the prepaids (or escrows) to that figure. Round the result down to the nearest multiple of $50.

For example, suppose you want to buy a $25,000 home utilizing FHA 221D-2 financing. How much loan could you get?

(1) $25,000   (appraised value)
   + $600 (closing costs—FHA schedule)
   ―――――――
    $25,600

(2) $25,600
   ×   .97
   ―――――――
    $24,832

(3) $24,832
   +   487   (estimated prepaids or escrows)
   ―――――――
    $25,319

    (4) $25,319 (rounded down to nearest multiple of $50 equals
            $25,300)

    (5) The largest loan amount is 100% of appraised value, so
          100% of $25,000 is $25,000. This is the loan amount.

WORKSHEETS

The following pages contain worksheets for computing financial costs you would encounter using 221D-2 financing.

Worksheet for FHA 221D-2 Loans

Buyer's Closing Costs = See the FHA schedule at the end of this chapter.

Loan Amount = (1) Appraised value + Closing Costs =

_____ (1)

(2) .97 *times* _____ (1) = _____ (2)

(3) _____ (2) + tax & insurance prepaids =

_____ (3)

(4) Round (3) down to nearest multiple of $50 to determine loan amount.

Down Payment = Sales Price of home *minus* loan amount.

Prepaids or Escrows

(1) Insurance = Phone your insurance agent; or a) $\dfrac{\text{sales price} +}{\$2,000}$ $3.00 = 1 month's insurance; then, b) 1 month's insurance *times* 13 months = escrow amount.

(2) Tax = Phone: owner, broker, or county assessor's office; then: *Divide* yearly taxes by 4 to get 3 months' figure. (Some lenders may require more than 3 months' escrow.)

(3) Interest = a) 1 year's interest = loan amount *times* interest rate; then, b) 1 year's interest *divided* by 12 = 1 month's interest.

Attorney's Fee = Phone your lawyer or local Bar Association. (Fee range: 1/2% to 1% of purchase price, or flat fee.)

Worksheet

Address : _____   Type of Loan : _____

Price : _____   Interest Rate : _____

Buyer's Closing Costs : _____

Loan Amount : _____

Down Payment : _____

Insurance Prepaids : _____

Tax Prepaids : _____

Interest Prepaids : _____

Attorney's Fee : _____

Total Costs Due
At Closing _____

Schedule of FHA Closing Costs

October 1985

Market Price of Property	Closing Costs
$20,000 through $20,999	$ 650
$21,000 " $22,599	$ 700
$22,600 " $24,249	$ 750
$24,250 " $25,199	$ 800
$25,200 " $27,999	$ 850
$28,000 " $31,999	$ 900
$32,000 " $35,999	$ 950
$36,000 " $39,999	$1,000
$40,000 " $44,999	$1,050
$45,000 " $48,999	$1,100
$49,000 " $52,999	$1,150
$53,000 " $56,999	$1,200
$57,000 " $61,999	$1,250
$62,000 " $65,999	$1,300
$66,000 " $69,999	$1,350
$70,000 " $74,999	$1,400
$75,000 " $78,999	$1,450
$79,000 " $82,999	$1,500
$83,000 and up	$1,550

*HUD Handbook 4150.1, Paragraph 3-62.

OTHER FHA PROGRAMS

The Department of Housing and Urban Development has a wide variety of programs, some of which may be of interest to you. The Section 203K program provides mortgage insurance to help families purchase, repair or improve, or refinance and improve existing one- to four-unit dwellings that are more than one year old. You can get one big loan to pay for the purchase price *and* the improvements! The maximum loan amount is the same as under the Section 203B program. Contact your local HUD field office for details.

If you are interested in purchasing a co-operative unit, then check into the Section 213 program. For potential condominium purchasers, I recommend that you discuss the Section 234 program with an approved lender.

The Urban Homesteading program has attracted lots of interest nationwide. This program transfers HUD, VA, or Farmer's Home Administration-owned homes to local governments. The local governments then sell the homes, sometimes for as low as one dollar, to individuals who must bring the home up to code standards within one year and also occupy the home for five years to receive title to the property.

Legislation in 1983 added Section 251, authorizing the FHA to insure adjustable-rate mortgages with the following features. The lender must explain the "worst case scenario" in writing to the borrower. Negative amortization is prohibited. Interest rate adjustments are to be made annually, and cannot exceed one percentage point per year. There is a cap on the interest rate; it cannot change more than five percentage points from the initial rate.

At HUD, new programs are developed and old programs are refined from time to time. If these programs interest you, stay in touch with HUD in your locale.

11
VA or GI Loans

If you or your spouse served in the armed services, read this section. If not, skip it! It does not apply to you.

The Veterans Administration (VA) loan is backed by a government guarantee to the lender to honor your note should you default. It is also referred to as a GI loan, because you must have served for the stated periods of time.

Which veterans are eligible? Eligibility hinges on two things:
(1) Your discharge must have been any kind other than a dishonorable one;
(2) You must have served on active duty for a certain number of days:
    (a) If you were in the service from September, 1940, to July 25, 1947, the requirement is 90 days' active duty;
    (b) From July 25, 1947, to June 27, 1950, the requirement is 181 days' active duty;
    (c) From June 28, 1950, to January 31, 1955, the requirement is 90 days' active duty;
    (d) From January 31, 1955, to post-Viet Nam, the requirement is 181 days' active duty.

ADVANTAGES OF THE VA LOAN

The down payment is a matter for the lender and GI buyer to negotiate. It is often zero! And, the loan closing costs, including the prepaid escrow items, may be paid in whole or part by the seller. In effect, a GI could conceivably move in virtually free! Lenders, as a practice, will negotiate some minimal down payment, as they feel it is desirable for the buyers to have something at stake.

As of late 1985, the maximum VA loan is $110,000. With a down payment, the maximum amount is $135,000. These figures are revised periodically.

HOW TO APPLY

When applying for a VA guaranteed loan, the veteran needs his DD 214 Form (separation form). Take this form to the lender you have decided to use. If you are an ex-GI, you are a fool not to seek further information about utilizing this benefit. To determine your exact situation, talk to your VA office or your lender.

12
Involving the Owner in Financing

Why would a seller want to play the role of a lender? There are several good reasons:

(1) The seller has not received any other offers for his home that are close to his desired price.

(2) The home is too old, in need of many repairs, or in a neighborhood that the lending institutions consider to be too risky.

(3) The owner does not need to receive a large bundle of cash at closing. He can afford to have the payments deferred.

(4) The owner views his decision to carry the mortgage as one that will provide him with steady monthly income. The loan is secured by the home itself, and the owner receives a very good rate of return that tops any other investment he could make. (Usually the interest rate is the same as the going conventional rate, or slightly higher. But, it is always up to the parties to negotiate!)

THE CONTRACT FOR DEED

The contract for deed is the first method an owner can utilize to finance the sale of his own home. In some states this is also called a "land contract," because it is often utilized in financing vacant land that institutional lenders usually avoid lending money on. It is also a common financing method for rural property, particularly midwestern farms.

Let us see how the contract for deed works in practice. You want to buy a home for $25,000, but at present do not have the money for a down payment and the other initial costs. Perhaps your income is not near the $1,000-a-month guideline either. The owner refuses to sell the home FHA, since it is in need of repairs; and he doesn't want those expenses, nor any additional financing charges at closing time.

What can you do? You can offer to give the seller a cash down payment, and agree to pay the balance in monthly installments.

How much down? How long a loan term? Since the owner is the lender, virtually *anything* goes! *Everything* is open for negotiation, and you do not have to meet any formulas at all. The owner just wants to be assured that you make enough to pay your installments. For example, offer the owner $1,000 down, and ask for a twenty-year note at 9 percent on the balance of the purchase price. That would be monthly payments of $216 to the owner. The contract should also specify who is responsible for taxes and insurance. (Usually the buyer is.)

When the contract is signed, the contract and deed are usually delivered to a third party. The third party holds them, acting as an escrow agent or trustee. This third party is instructed to deliver the deed to the buyer after all, or a specified portion, of the loan balance is paid by the buyer to the seller. This practice of letting a third party hold the deed is to guarantee delivery to the buyer at the proper time. Should the seller die while holding the deed himself, the buyer could get involved in a real mess with the estate. Another potential nightmare would be chasing after one of the sellers, should they get divorced or move to another city. Your contract for the deed should be recorded, as a general rule. The contract is an instrument that affects title. Talk with your lawyer about this matter.

FURTHER VARIATIONS

Often, a seller will finance the purchase for five years, with the stipulation that the buyer refinance the loan with a regular loan from an institution.

Most contracts for a deed contain language that purports to define what happens should the buyer miss a payment. The typical language states that "time is of the essence"; and should the buyer miss a payment, the seller may declare a forfeiture and all rights of the purchaser are terminated. The buyer's payments will be treated as rents and liquidated damages, should the buyer default. The seller is often given the right of re-entry. Another form the language might employ would be to give the seller the option to declare the total balance to be due upon default or late payments, or to foreclose at the seller's option.

What are the rights of both parties upon default or late payment? To be quite frank, different jurisdictions treat these problems in different ways. Most courts will treat contract for deeds or land contracts as equitable mortgages, and give the buyer a specified period of time to redeem the property. Other courts may require a public sale with the buyer and seller sharing the proceeds in an equitable way, and a few might even construe the contract strictly.

LEGAL AID IS A MUST!

If you are going to use a contract for deed (land contract) as the financing vehicle, see a lawyer *before* you sign the contract. Your attorney can explain your state's laws regarding land contracts and advise you of all the legal ramifications.

The contract for your property should be recorded in the office of the county clerk. Before any document can be recorded, it must comply with certain formalities. (Example: signed by all parties and acknowledged.) Such a record protects you from a dishonest or mistaken escrow agent who may transfer the deed to the wrong people, or have the deed stolen and subsequently transferred.

In summary, you can see that the contract for deed (land contract) has several advantages for the purchaser, namely: 1) lower down payments; 2) no loan origination fees, closing costs, private mortgage insurance premiums, or escrows; 3) no rigid loan qualification standards; 4) any interest rates and loan terms that you can negotiate.

The disadvantages of contracts for deed are the uncertain legal rights that accompany such arrangements.

USE OF SECOND MORTGAGES

A second mortgage is subordinated to the rights of the first mortgage holder who has properly recorded his interest.

Suppose you want to buy a $30,000 home. Your offer has been accepted, and you have qualified for an 80 percent conventional loan. You calculate that by the time you pay all the closing costs and incur moving expenses, you will be short $1,500. You ask the owner to loan you the $1,500, and you sign a note and give the seller a mortgage. (Security interest in the property should you break your promise to pay.) The owner's second mortgage is entitled to consideration in the event of default, but only after the prior first mortgage ($24,000) is fully discharged by the lending institution.

Why would a seller do this for you? Because your offer may be the best or only offer he received! The seller doesn't wish to blow the sale just because he doesn't want to wait a while to receive a small portion of his proceeds.

Be creative in financing! Where there's a will—there's a way!

THE PURCHASE-MONEY MORTGAGE

A second method of owner-financing is the purchase-money mortgage. It operates in essentially the same manner as the contract for deed, but with one major difference—the buyer gets the deed at closing! The buyer makes a down payment, and signs a note for the loan at specified terms. The seller takes back a mortgage.

What happens in case of default? The seller *must* institute foreclosure proceedings. The seller cannot merely re-enter the property. The buyer will be given the right of redemption. Should the home sell at a public auction, the seller/lender would receive the unpaid balance of the loan, and the buyer would receive any surplus funds.

Try to use the purchase-money mortgage in owner financed transactions. Don't be afraid to use the contract for deed, but only as a second choice. Always use a lawyer.

ASSUMING EXISTING LOANS

Once in a great while you hear someone bragging about assuming an older loan at 4½ percent or some such staggering rate. Let me explain how assumptions work. Suppose you wish to buy a home for $30,000. The home was built four years ago at a cost of $20,000. The owner originally got 90 percent financing at 7¾ percent for thirty years. His present loan balance is $16,500. The owner's equity is, therefore, $13,500.

What if you, the buyer, wanted to assume the mortgage and remaining payments for twenty-six years? That is, you want to stand in the same shoes the seller does with his loan. You must do the following things: (1) pay the seller $13,500; (2) be approved by the lender in most cases, providing the loan can be assumed; (3) pay the lender a loan transfer fee in most cases.

As you can see, the assumption of existing loans often requires large cash outlays to pay the owner his equity. Our bragging buddy who assumed at 4½ percent loan failed to tell us how much cash he had to put out for the owner's equity. That interest rate suggests that the loan was made in the mid-fifties. Since that time, the owner has surely built up sizeable equity through both payments to reduce principal and real estate appreciation in his area.

Understand that whether or not a loan can be assumed is to be judged by the terms of the original loan. To find out this information, you have to phone the seller's lender. The lender will tell you if the loan may be assumed and what is the policy on assumption. Is the interest rate the same, or can the lender adjust it? Is there a fee for this assumption or loan transfer? Must the buyer "qualify" and meet certain requirements of the lender? Does the lender require the buyer to have enough money to pay the owner without additional loans being incurred? The only way to find out all the answers is to ask the lender.

Assumptions are almost always allowed on existing FHA or VA loans. On other loans, look for small owner equities or no qualification rules by the lender.

13

Buying, Building, or Financing a New Home

Are there any *big* worries about financing? Not really! You need only one home loan, sufficient to assist you in paying the purchase price. The construction costs, etc., are the burden of the builder/developer. A variety of financing devices may be employed by the builder, but you worry only about one loan. You may utilize FHA, VA, or conventional financing.

A few pointers on buying into new developments:

(1) The location is critical, as in the selection of older homes. Property values in adjacent neighborhoods are extremely important to you.

(2) Who is the developer or builder? Find out all you can about them, and their past efforts. Have their other projects appreciated well? Are owners of their past projects happy with the quality? You might ask some tradesmen working on Home A, being built by Builder A, what they think about the quality of Homes B, C, and D that other builders are doing. In Home B you reverse the process.

(3) Observe the quality of workmanship yourself. You are smart to inspect the home in various stages of construction. If you only see the finished product, the frosting may cover up any defects in the cake. Use your eyes and common sense to check everything and ask the workers questions. If you have a friend in one of the trades, perhaps he will come along with you some Sunday. (Rarely will anyone be working on Sunday, so you can inspect at a leisurely pace.)

(4) Check to see if the builder offers some financing gimmick! Sometimes builders will pay your closing costs as an enticement to buy.

BUILDING A NEW HOME

What about buying a lot and building your own home? This is an appealing idea to many, because you can design your "dream house." Also, you can save a good chunk of money by acting as your own contractor, if you have the knowledge or help to do so. There are many headaches of the non-financial variety that you want to avoid. Some of them are:

(1) Is the lot zoned for the type of home you plan to build?
(2) Do you have good working plans for the construction of the home? Do you need an architect? Do your plans meet all the requirements of local codes?
(3) What about the other homes in the area, built or yet to be built—will they affect appreciation adversely? Is the floor plan conducive to resale should you later sell the home?
(4) Have you selected reputable tradesmen or contractors to do the work? Have you viewed their past building efforts? Are the other owners happy with the quality of their new homes?

Tread very slowly in these matters, using the advice of lenders and others.

FINANCING NEW CONSTRUCTION

Let us suppose your mind is firmly set on building a new house. So what do you need to know about financing?

First of all, let us nail down the terminology.

A construction loan is called an "interim-financing loan." The life or term of this loan is generally nine months to a year, the maximum time expected for the completion of construction.

A "permanent loan," sometimes called a final loan, is placed upon the building and property after completion. This operates just like a mortgage loan on an existing home.

In essence then, we are dealing with two distinct loans. Both loans may be available from the same lender, or it may be to your advantage to get interim financing from an institution, preferably one that specializes in construction loans. Then you could seek permanent financing elsewhere.

Where does one go for new-construction loans? The best bets are savings and loan institutions or banks. But not all lenders will consider a construction loan. Why? Because there are too many risks and supervisory tasks involved that require expertise.

Some of the risks inherent in new-construction loans that make the lender "gun-shy" are: cost estimates are too low, laborers or craftsmen go on strike, or the contractor goes bankrupt. Also, construction must be periodically inspected before paying portions of the costs to the building contractor.

Shed no tears for the lenders, though. Actually, the smarter and hungrier lenders know they can make a good buck by filling this need for financing. They protect themselves in the following ways:

(1) The interest rates may be slightly higher for interim loans than for permanent loans.

(2) The loan ratio is reduced in comparison to a normal, permanent loan. The loan ratios run between 70 and 85 percent of the estimated value of your projected home. The stronger your financial condition is, the higher your loan percentage will be. But don't expect to be luckier than 85 percent. Looked at another way, you will have to put up 15 to 30 percent of the cash as a down payment or initial investment of your own!

(3) The big catch-all is labelled interim-financing "service fees." Expect to pay one to three points to compensate the lender for his supervision and risk sharing.

As I mentioned earlier, some lenders may specialize in interim financing. But most often, a lender will try to hook you for both the interim and permanent financing. They normally offer you some package deal that features the beginning of an amortized mortgage right after construction is completed. The interest rate may differ from the interim-financing rate.

Once you have shopped lenders, you need to submit a loan application for interim financing. Besides your personal financial and income statements, the lender will also want the plans and specifications for your homesite, the contractor's name, a copy of any agreement you have made with them, and the estimates of cost.

What happens after loan approval? Construction begins. We then consider three questions: Who is paid; How are they paid; When are they paid?

First of all, the lender writes the checks. The lender can pay either the contractor (who portions out payments to subcontractors), or the lender can pay the suppliers, laborers and craftsmen directly.

When are these payments made? There are various systems and schedules. A few lenders pay the costs as they occur. The widespread practice, however, is to make three to six periodic payments. These payments are made upon the completion of certain specified construction stages, such as: roofing, plumbing, interior walls, basement floor, finished flooring, etc.

Each lender prefers a particular schedule or method. The lender makes inspections before these payments are granted. Almost all lenders will hold back about 15 to 20 percent of the loan value for a couple of months after construction is completed. This is done to be sure that all the liens of subcontractors have been removed and the little odds and ends have been finished after the occupants move in.

Building your own home can be a great thing, but you must realize the time and costs involved, so you avoid any financial surprises.

14

What You Need to Know about Mortgage Shopping and Loan Applications

After your offer has been accepted, you must try to get the type of loan specified in your contract. What do you do? Let your fingers do the walking, like the ads say. Use the telephone to shop for mortgage terms just as you would shop for lawn furniture.

The type of loan you want determines whom you call first. If you want an FHA or VA loan, call a savings and loan or a private mortgage lender, who can usually be identified by names like Morgan Mortgage Company or Laughlin Loan Co. Banks do not make FHA loans or VA loans.

If you are seeking a conventional loan, banks may be able to help you. Savings and loan associations are the major source, and you can also get conventional financing from insurance companies, mortgage companies, and loan companies.

When shopping for FHA or VA loans, remember that interest rates and closing costs are set by the government; so no matter who you call, these will be the same. The only variance will be in the income needed to qualify and the debt analysis. Also, points that the *seller* has to pay can vary. (Remember, the buyer can pay only one point!)

Conventional loan makers are subject to the basic rules of supply and demand, so their programs and policies vary. Conventional loan amounts vary from 70 to 95 percent of the appraised value of the property to be bought. The loan percentage is a decision for the lender to make. Ninety-five percent is the maximum loan amount, providing it is insured by Private Mortgage Insurance (PMI).

INTEREST RATES VARY

What do different interest rates mean to you in terms of money? You can compare monthly payments on principal and interest by looking up the payments that correspond to the loan amount and quoted interest rate. A mortgage payment guide is included in Chapter 19 of this book (pp. 125-41). For example, a $25,000 loan at 13 percent for thirty years would cost you $276.55 a month, exclusive of any escrows. At 15 percent, monthly payments would be $316.11; and at 16 percent your payment would be $336.19 monthly. Check this table now! Do you understand how to use it?

SHOPPING TO CUT YOUR INITIAL COSTS

Although saving a few bucks a month on interest rates is nothing to sneeze at, the big savings can be found in the variation in initial costs you will be required to pay at closing. These costs include down payments, loan origination fee, and closing costs. These costs are one-time-only costs. However, they can add up to a big lump sum. You can cut down the size of this initial cost by shrewd shopping.

EXAMPLES AND ANALYSIS

Suppose again that you want to buy a $50,000 home. The owner tells you that he will not accept an FHA loan, so you must try to get a conventional loan, as the contract provides for. The contract calls for a minimum of 85 percent conventional financing. You start by phoning your area savings and loan associations, mortgage and loan companies, and banks. Ask to speak with a loan officer.

Your calls give you the following information:

(1) Slusser Savings and Loan Association offers you a thirty-year loan at 11 percent interest, including PMI. Loan fee is two points, and closing costs are estimated at $400. They offer a 90 percent loan.

(2) Hartley Home Mortgage Company offers you a thirty-year loan at 11½ percent interest, including PMI. Loan fee is

five points, and closing costs are estimated at $350. They offer a 95 percent loan.

(3) Nielson-Tardiff Loan Company offers you a thirty-year loan at 10¾ percent interest, including PMI. Loan fee is zero, and closing costs are estimated at $300. They offer an 85 percent loan.

Let's analyze these three different financing arrangements.

(1) Slusser Savings and Loan's offer translates into the following numbers: The loan amount would be $45,000; monthly payments (principal + interest) would be $429, plus 78 escrows = $507 a month; and you would need a gross monthly income of $2,028 a month to qualify. The initial costs include: a) down payment of 10% = $5,000; b) loan origination fee = $900; c) closing costs of $400. The total initial costs would be $6,300 at Slusser Savings and Loan. (We assume that the prepaids will be the same at each institution, that is, $78 per month.)

(2) Hartley Home Mortgage Company's offer translates into the following numbers: The loan amount would be $47,500; monthly payments would be $470 (principal + interest), plus 78 escrows = $548; and you would need a gross monthly income of $2,192 to qualify. The initial costs include: a) down payment of 5% = $2,500; b) loan origination fee = $2,375; c) closing costs are $350. The total of these initial costs is $5,225.

(3) Nielson-Tardiff's offer translates into the following numbers: The loan amount would be $42,500; monthly payments would be $397 + 78 escrows = $475; and you would need a gross monthly income of $1,900 to qualify. The initial costs include: a) down payment of 15% = $7,500; b) loan origination fee = zero; c) closing costs are $300. The total of these initial costs is $7,800.

As you can see, offer number three gives you the lowest monthly payments and easiest qualifying income figure. But offer number two saves you over $1,075 due at closing compared to offer number one; and saves you $2,575 compared to offer number three.

So you must choose between minimizing present initial costs due at closing and minimizing monthly payments and loan amount.

Given this choice, most people would choose the smaller initial costs. Why? First, they may lack the cash to pay higher initial costs at closing. Second, they may need this cash to pay for the moving van or redecorating, etc.; and finally, a lower initial investment will maximize leverage.

After you analyze the different mortgage offers, pick the one that meets your financial situation best. Then, get back on the phone and call the same person that you talked to earlier. Make an appointment to see him or her as soon as possible, before the terms quoted to you on the phone change.

USING THE PHONE FOR MORTGAGE SHOPPING

(1) Phone the institution . . . ask to speak with a loan officer about a home loan.

(2) Identify yourself . . . ask the officer's name . . . write it down.

(3) State your purpose—you want some information about the lender's policies and terms.

(4) Give the location of the home you wish to buy, the purchase price, and the age of the home.

(5) Tell the loan officer what your monthly gross income is . . . also tell him/her your monthly debts that are more than six months in term.

(6) Be sure you ask what the highest loan percentage you could get is.

(7) Thank the loan officer for his/her time. Say that you will phone a few more lenders for quotes, and that you will call back and specifically ask for him or her should you decide to deal with that particular institution.

VISITING THE LENDER

What happens when you apply for a home loan? Generally, you are first given a form to fill out. In this form, the lender gets information about you and the property you wish to buy. The lender, in turn, gives you information about the lending policies, lending programs, and terms that his institution offers you. Remember, lenders are in business to lend you money. So they are happy to see you! You might be money in their pocket.

From the lender's viewpoint, there are two basic areas of in-they are interested in the property and home you ... to buy, since it will be used as security for the proposed loan to you. Although you will be asked a few questions about the home you wish to buy, the loan officer you are speaking with rarely, if ever, even sees the property. A professional appraisal will be made of the property, and the results will be given to the lender. You will be charged a non-refundable fee of $50 to $75 for this.

Secondly, the lender is interested in *you!* Specifically, he is interested in your debt-paying habits, and your future earnings and ability to meet future debts. To this end, the lender needs employment and credit information. More about this:

(1) Credit information is essential to the lender to help him assess your past habits in dealing with other lenders. The lender will ask for your written permission to have credit-rating agencies investigate your past dealings. You may also be asked to list some personal references. Be sure to notify the people you list as references, to avoid any surprises. Give them plenty of advance notice to think about what a great person you are.

(2) The lender wants to verify your personal income at the present time, check on your reliability on the job, check on job stability, and estimate your future income. There are two frequently asked questions about loans: Does the lender consider a woman's earnings? What about bonuses and commissions? Law requires that women receive equal consideration in lending. Regarding additions to your income (like overtime pay), if these additions occur on a regular basis they will be considered. Usually, the lenders will merely require a statement from the employers about these extras and how regularly they occur.

HOW TO HANDLE A PERSONAL INTERVIEW

When being interviewed, you will be subjectively sized up! Your incentives, goals, knowledge, sincerity, and capabilities will be evaluated. The conversation is about you. You are asked to explain or amplify some of the written information.

You also discuss terms of the loan. Understand that negotiation is proper. For example, the lender may want to give you a 75 percent loan, but you want an 80 percent loan. Understand that the more you invest in the home, the happier the lender is (because his margin of safety is greater). Also, the size of your down payment allegedly reflects the seriousness of your purpose and psychological commitment.

Sometimes, you may be considered a marginal applicant, perhaps due to your income, or past debts, or because the property you wish to buy needs many repairs or is in an area the lender is uncertain about. Lenders may require additional security in the forms of security interests in other real estate or stocks you own, or perhaps a co-signer(s) on the note.

15
Making Offers and Writing Contracts: What the Layman Needs to Know

You have found a nice home in a nice area. You are interested in the home, and want to make an offer to purchase it. Your offering price depends upon three things: (1) local market conditions; (2) the seller's motives; (3) your own motives.

IDENTIFYING THE MARKET

How can you tell what kind of market conditions prevail? It is all a question of supply and demand, and marketing time. It is a buyer's market if the number of homes for sale (supply) exceeds the number of people who are serious potential home buyers (demand). It is a seller's market if the number of buyers (demand) exceeds the (supply) number of homes available for sale.

Competitive markets are fairly balanced in terms of supply-and-demand equality.

If you are not sophisticated enough to determine this yourself through competitive shopping, you can check with local lenders or real estate brokers to get their opinions. There are mini-markets within the local markets. For example, the demand for homes in the $35,000 to $50,000 range might far exceed supply; whereas demand for $80,000 homes may be significantly lower than the supply of homes offered for sale in the current market.

BROKERS CAN HELP

Real estate professionals can be the best people to assess the market, as they have access to the vital data. Many areas have co-operative services that allow all participating brokers to work together to sell each other's listings and split the commission. These services are often called multiple listing services. They also collect data on all the homes listed, bought and sold, and the length of time they were on the market. Sophisticated multiple listing groups use computers to provide them with useful data.

For example, a computer can be programmed to print out data that the broker requests for a given square-mile area. The computer can print out a list of available homes in the desired price range, or those homes with four bedrooms, or those homes with two-car garages, or fireplaces, etc. In this respect, the computer can do all the legwork and research.

In terms of valuable data about market conditions, brokers can tell you the average selling time for homes in a given price range, so you can determine if there is a rapid turnover. Lenders also keep these types of statistics, but not about homes currently for sale. They, like brokers, have data about homes that have already been sold.

Naturally, if it is a buyer's market, you can afford to reduce the price offered in most cases. But only after considering the other two factors.

YOUR OWN MOTIVES

Just how badly do you want this home? Are you pressed for time? Does your apartment lease expire soon? Have you searched and searched and grown tired of the hunt? Is this house really super, and your spouse would never forgive you if you blow the negotiations?

Remember, keep the numbers in perspective! By this I mean put yourself in the shoes of the seller, too. What does a $1,000 price reduction mean to him? Consider this: to *you* it will not be a lump sum due at closing. To *him* it will be a lump sum he will not receive at closing.

Consider what $1,000 means to you: Spread over your thirty-year loan at, say 9 percent, $1,000 is $8 a month. Eight dollars! Using a technique professional sellers call "the reduction to the ridiculous," we reduce that to two dollars a week, or about 28¢ a day! Heck, you might spend that on cigarettes! You could save two bucks a week by taking your lunch to work once a week!

THE SELLER'S POSITION

Why is the seller offering his home for sale? This is a crucial question! Does the seller have to move to another city because of a job transfer? Is the house too small for a growing family? Is it too large for an aging couple whose children have left the roost? Is the seller just testing the market out, selling only if someone offers him an extravagant price for his home?

Time is a key consideration! Is the seller in a hurry to sell and get his money out of this house? Does he need the proceeds to finance his next home purchase? Does he have to move to a new place before the schools open?

You should be able to determine the seller's motive by conversation with the sellers, their broker, or the local neighbors. Sometimes sellers don't want people to know why they are selling, as they perceive such knowledge could diminish their bargaining position. Consequently, their lips are sealed.

THE PSYCHOLOGY OF NEGOTIATION

The seller may have received a few or many offers before you decided to put in an offer. If you can find out the range of offers previously refused, you will have a good picture of the seller's mind. Sometimes, a broker will tell you what price the seller considers unacceptable.

When you are dealing with a broker, you have a third party to negotiate and soften the words between two parties with the same objective: to make the best deal for themselves. Brokers bear the brunt of cross words and angry faces. Negotiations through brokers have a higher chance of success, because of individuals' egos. Again, consider the seller's viewpoint. The seller's home is an extension of his personality. You may tell him that you think the color scheme is atrocious. He might have spent four days of his vacation doing the work. Your objections may be taken personally, in other words. Inevitably, they usually are!

When you and the seller deal directly, you run a higher risk of alienating each other, and blowing the deal. You find it hard to follow up rejected offers with new offers, since it would appear that you are too anxious. Basically, buyer and seller each expect to give a little and get a little. *Remember This:* Don't strip the other guy of all his pride!

How do you give a little and take a little? Suppose you want to make an offer on a home listed for $45,000. But your judgment says it's worth only $43,000. You offer $43,000 and the seller rejects. You then offer the full $45,000, but include in the offer conditions that the owner paint the living room, fix the back porch steps, put three more inches of insulation in the attic, and leave the refrigerator. Get the idea? You toss the ball to the seller, and he can punt, pass or kick. Or counter-offer.

Some buyers follow formulas for price negotiations, such as the first offer should be 10 percent off the listing price, or maybe 5 percent or 7 percent. I think that is nonsense, unless you are merely shopping for bargains. Only you can evaluate the three key criteria, and give them a weighting in your own mind.

HOW TO MAKE AN OFFER

First, understand that contracts for the sale of real property must be in writing to be enforceable. This is a legal requirement to prevent fraud. Oral contracts are not enforceable for sales of homes.

Therefore, your offer to purchase must be in writing! Mere *negotiations* may, of course, be conducted verbally. Remember this: When you make an offer, you have created the power of acceptance in the seller. Should the seller accept your offer, you have a binding contract. So, do not make another offer on another home, while you still have an offer on a first home that has not been accepted or rejected in writing by the seller. If you did make several offers on several homes, you have created several powers of acceptance, and could very well wind up buying two or more homes! Don't laugh—this happens!

What do you write your offer on? Usually one of two instruments is used: 1) a binder, or 2) a form contract. You may bring your own forms, or the seller or broker or lawyer may produce some. The "binder" is used in many states, in accordance with local customs of brokers and lawyers. The binder states the basic terms of the sale, and then the parties seek legal help from lawyers to draw up the final formal documents. Despite some assurances that this binder is "merely a preliminary document that means nothing," be careful! It is a *binding* legal contract! Visit your attorney first, and get a form from him or her.

The use of a form contract is usually preferable to the use of binders. Brokers have vast supplies of form contracts; office supply stores usually carry them; and the parties can get them from their lawyers. Be safe! Follow your lawyer's advice.

EARNEST DEPOSITS

What about "down payments" and "earnest deposits"? The terminology is often interchanged.

You make down payments at closings, not to sellers or trust agents. Down payments are a matter for the lender and buyer to decide.

An earnest deposit is merely something with which to tease the seller and to show him that your offer is serious! This deposit is important to the seller, because he will take his home off the market while you try to get financing, as the contract calls for. This normally takes three weeks, and other conditions may take two or three more weeks. So the seller loses valuable marketing time.

Brokers love high earnest money deposits because, should you back out of a valid contract, they have something to go after in payment from the seller for their commission. The seller would also have this money to treat as damages for his losses.

There is no required earnest deposit. Use your own judgment! Don't tie up any more funds than you wish. Some unexpected bills may come your way. A couple of hundred dollars is quite sufficient. Even nothing will do, if nothing is all you want to offer! The seller may have similar offers from other parties, and could judge your relative financial strengths by incomes. So, you could be adversely affected by the paucity of your earnest deposit.

CONTRACTS FOR THE SALE OF REAL ESTATE

As mentioned earlier, there are many different forms in use. However, these standard forms all have the same basic elements, plus or minus a few frills. Here is a survey of what you can expect these forms to contain:

(1) **Sale and Identification Information**
This is usually the first thing contracts cover. The buyers and sellers are named, and their intention to transfer real property is stated.

(2) **Land and All Property Being Sold**
The land is named by its legal description. The house and other structures (garage, tool shed, etc.) are referred to as "all improvements" on the land. The personal property involved in the sale is specifically defined (Example: refrigerator, washer and dryer). Certain property may be specifically excluded from the sale, such as a crystal chandelier that Grandma gave the sellers for their wedding.

(3) **Type of Deed**
There are four common types of deeds and numerous special-purpose deeds. The four common types are: a) the general warranty deed; b) the quitclaim deed; c) the special warranty deed; d) and the bargain and sale deed. In almost all circumstances you want a *general warranty deed!* This is work for your attorney.

(4) **Purchase Price**
The total purchase price is stated. The earnest deposit is stated and noted to be partial payment, with the remainder to be paid upon delivery of deed at closing, unless otherwise provided.

(5) **Financing Conditions**
States which type of financing buyer wants to use. If a loan is needed, the type is *specified* and so is the interest rate, loan length, loan fees, points, etc. Should the buyer fail to be granted a loan of the exact type specified, the contract is null and void. The buyer is given a certain amount of time to get the loan approved, usually three to four weeks in most areas. Also spelled out is which party is responsible for which escrows and closing costs.

(6) **Title**
After loan approval, seller has a certain number of days to furnish the buyer with a certified abstract of title and a current UCC search certificate. The buyer has a certain time to examine the title and state any objections. A certain time is allowed to clear any objections to title.

(7) **Taxes**
This provision generally calls for seller to pay all special

assessments, and the current *ad valorem* taxes are pro-
rated between the buyer and seller.

(8) **Liens on the Property**
Seller must pay in full any existing liens on the property
before closing. (Example: labor or material liens.)

(9) **Termite Clause**
Seller usually pays for the termite inspection. There are
two basic types of certificates that termite companies
give: a) states that property is free of visible termite
infestation; b) free of infestation plus visible termite
damage. Ask for the second.

(10) **Condition of the Property**
This clause normally states that: All the fixtures and
equipment and systems shall be in normal working order
at date of closing. If repairs are needed, which party pays
is defined.

(11) **Closing Date Is Named**

(12) **Breach of Contract**
This clause defines the consequences to a party that fails
to live up to the terms of the contract.

(13) **Special Conditions**
This is a "catch-all" section, reserved for any items you
desire that have not been covered by any other part of
the contract. (Example: seller will fix the back steps and
paint the bathroom with navy blue enamel.)

16
Creative Financing and New Mortgages

Almost half of all home sales in the past few years utilized some sort of *seller* financing. Chapter 12 explains the basics of owner financing, and offers legal and financial advice. The following pages supplement that material, and introduce you to some of the latest wrinkles in the evolving market.

BUY-DOWNS

Have you ever browsed through the real estate section in the Sunday paper and spotted a builder's ad offering 8 percent* interest rates on financing? Your first reaction is, "This must be a mistake! Interest rates are 14 percent everywhere else!" Then you notice the asterisk and read a footnote explaining that the 8 percent interest is only for the first year of your loan. After that, your monthly payments increase to the usual amount necessary to amortize the loan at 14 percent. The home builder or seller offers what is known as an interest-rate "buy-down." The builder "buys-down" the interest rate from 14 to 8 percent by making up the difference in payment to the lender.

Suppose you borrow $50,000 at 14 percent for thirty years, but the seller offers to buy-down the interest rate to 8 percent in the first year. Your payments in that first year will be $366.89 a month, while the seller would pay $225.55 monthly to the lender. The lender would receive a total monthly payment of $592.44.

In effect, the seller partially "subsidizes" the buyer's monthly loan payments. This subsidy totals $2,706.60 for the first year. In the second year the buyer is on his own, and makes the full monthly payments of $592.44 on the conventional loan. Why doesn't the

seller just reduce the price of the home by $2,706.60? A price reduc-
tion would have little effect on your monthly payments and do little
to solve the affordability problem that you may face.

Are there any regulations on these buy-downs? How big can the
buy-down be? Five percent? Ten percent? Fifteen percent? How
many years can a buy-down be in effect? Five years or longer? Only
the buyer and seller can answer these questions in a contract. In
other words, these items are all open to negotiation. How nice for
you!

VARIATIONS OF THE BASIC BUY-DOWN

Creative financing is a lot like making your own ice-cream sundae:
The possibilities are endless! Consider these variations of the basic
buy-down. If you want a $50,000 loan, but can't afford to pay the
going market rate of 14 percent, a creative buy-down could be the
answer. In the first year you pay 8 percent interest; in the second
year you pay 10 percent; in the third year you pay 12 percent; and in
the fourth year the subsidy ends, thus you make full payments at 14
percent. This arrangement by the subsidizing seller would coincide
with your escalating salary and financial ability to meet the full
monthly payments.

A REPAYABLE BUY-DOWN

Here's another scenario that may work for you. Why not suggest
to your parents or a seller a repayable buy-down loan? For a $50,000
loan at 14 percent, you could suggest a two-year buy-down to 8
percent. The total subsidy would be $5,413.20, while your monthly
payments for two years would be $366.89.

A SLEEPY BUY-DOWN

When do you start repaying this subsidy? Stipulate in the note
that you make no payments on principal or interest until the beginning of the third year. This buy-down agreement would give you
some financial breathing room. You could even give the subsidizing
seller (or parents) a second mortgage to provide them with more
security than just the note.

SLEEPY-SECOND MORTGAGES

The use of second mortgages (or deeds of trust, as mortgages are called in some states) is explained in Chapter 12. Since all the terms of a second mortgage are negotiable, you can tailor the contract to your needs. For example, suppose you want to buy a $70,000 home, but can qualify only for a $50,000 loan. You have $7,000 to put down, so you need $13,000 more.

You realize that the seller has a loan balance of $20,000, but the loan cannot be assumed. The seller says he will carry a second mortgage for $13,000 at 13 percent for thirty years. You discover that you cannot afford to simultaneously make two monthly payments of $553.10 on your $50,000 loan and $143.81 on the second loan of $13,000. What can you do?

Try this proposal: Tell the seller that you will make no payments at all on the $13,000 loan until the fourth year. At that time you will pay off the entire loan by either selling the home or refinancing the loans. Such an arrangement is called a "sleepy-second" mortgage, because it sleeps for a while and wakes up four years later upon sale or mandatory refinancing.

Would a seller do this for you? Yes, if he or she needs to sell the home, and you are the only prospect. After all, the seller would walk away from this transaction with $37,000 in cash plus your note for $13,000 at 13 percent that is payable in four years.

BALLOON MORTGAGES

Any mortgage that requires the borrower to repay the entire debt before all the principal has been fully amortized is called a "balloon" mortgage. Suppose you need to borrow $80,000 to finance the purchase of a house. A savings and loan association will give you a loan of only $60,000 at 13 percent for thirty years, with monthly payments of $663.72.

The seller agrees to give you a second mortgage for $20,000 at 13 percent, but only for three years, which would require monthly payments of $673.88. Payments on both loans would cost you $1,337.60 a month—a figure you cannot afford. Do you have any alternatives?

You could tell the seller that you want a loan term of thirty years, not three years, but you will insert a clause in the note that says the entire loan is due and payable at the end of the third year. Your monthly payments on this second mortgage would be $221.24, a sum much more affordable than $673.88! After the third year you must either sell or refinance, because your final payment on the second loan swells (or "balloons") to the entire remaining principal balance.

INTEREST-ONLY BALLOONS

An interest-only balloon is a variation of the balloon mortgage, which calls for monthly payments that cover only the interest due on the loan, with no payment on the principal required until the final (balloon) payment is due. Interest-only balloon mortgages rarely exceed five years in term.

EQUITY SHARING

Potential home buyers who do not have enough money to make the necessary down payment and/or lack the earnings capacity to meet the monthly payments may ask a third party for help.

This third-party investor could pay some or all of the initial costs as well as the monthly expenses. In return for this financial aid, the investor will share in some percentage of the equity and appreciation. The investor normally is the co-owner of the home, and his or her name may also appear on the mortgage and note with that of the lender. Tax advantages similar to those for landlords flow to the investor.

Who are some investors likely to help *you* out? Why not approach your parents or relatives with a sound financial proposal that benefits both you and them?

I recommend that two clauses be inserted in your partnership agreement with the investor: 1) a clause that states that the resident/partner(s) must sell or refinance the loan before x years (3–5 years?); and 2) a clause that gives the resident/partner(s) the preemptive right to buy out the investor/partner(s) before the date requiring refinancing.

LAND LEASE

Since the land itself typically represents 20–25 percent of the purchase price, why not buy the home, but *lease* the land for ninety-nine years? Your monthly lease payments could be very low initially, or even include some portion of the payment that is applied to purchasing the land. This agreement would cut your down payment by 20–25 percent, and lower your monthly payments also!

LEASE WITH AN OPTION TO PURCHASE

You've found the perfect home and it's for sale! But you cannot get the necessary financing to buy it, and you're heartbroken. If you are really at a dead end financially, the lease with an option to buy is your last chance. Ask the seller if he or she would rent the home to you for a specified period (eighteen months, for example), and give you an option to purchase the home anytime before the lease expires.

This arrangement would allow you to move into your home now, with a very small initial investment. It also gives you more time to save money, get another job, or line up some financing. The only disadvantage is that you are still paying rent and receiving no tax benefits of ownership.

The owner retains title, gets the tax considerations of a landlord, and retains equity in the home which is off the market for the lease period.

LEASING CONSIDERATIONS

Let's talk about some practical considerations. First, how much should the rent be? Obviously, the owner must cover the mortgage payments and upkeep expenses. A guideline that is still valid in many areas is that monthly rent should be 1 percent of the market value of the home. For example, a $50,000 home should rent for $500. Also, because the owner may not be too keen on the idea initially, you may have to offer a premium rental amount or a large option fee. Should you pay the extra premium? You'll have to answer that one, because it depends on how badly you want a particular home!

Second, an option offer or contract must be supported by consideration to be legally valid. You may have to pay some option money to the seller, if the option agreement is separate from the rental agreement. Will this option money apply to your down payment? Not unless your contract says so!

Third, decide on a purchase price in the option agreement that would allow you to buy. I suggest a clause calling for an independent appraisal by a professional selected by both parties be included in the contract. This could be important because your ability to get maximum financing on the home will depend upon the lender's appraised value, as well as your earnings capacity.

A situation could develop where the seller insists on $55,000 for the home, but the lender's appraisal is only $50,000. If the lender will loan you a maximum of 90 percent of appraised value, your maximum loan will be $45,000. This means you need $10,000 down, not just $5,000! That could put an end to your deal, and your option money may not be recoverable either. Be sure to utilize the skills of professionals when drafting a lease-purchase option agreement.

MORTGAGES FOR THE LATE 1980s

Inflation has made the fixed-rate conventional home loan less widespread. Because fixed interest rates in inflationary times erode the value of the lender's principal, legislative changes in the early 1980s enabled savings and loans and banks with national charters to offer new types of home mortgage loans. This chapter will help you understand these "alphabet soup" mortgages and highlight their relative advantages and disadvantages.

LOANS WITH ADJUSTABLE INTEREST RATES

There are a wide variety of loans available that feature periodic adjustments in the rate of interest charged to the borrower. Some of these hybrids are the variable rate mortgage (VRM), renegotiated rate mortgage (RRM), rollover mortgage, adjustable rate mortgage (ARM), and the adjustable mortgage loan (AML).

The salient feature common to all these varieties is the adjustable nature of the interest rates. These mortgages may differ widely on the following items:

(1) How *often* may periodic adjustments of interest rates take place?

(2) How *many* adjustments may occur over the life of the loan?

(3) Is there a *limit* on interest rate increases?

(4) Are changes in interest rates *indexed* to some reliable measure of interest rates, like U.S. Treasury bill yields?

As a buyer, you need to compare the specifics of each mortgage program with your other financing alternatives. *Don't assume that all adjustable interest-rate loans are alike!* Besides differing on the previous four items, down payments, points, and qualifying standards will vary from lender to lender. (See Chapter 14 on mortgage shopping to hone your ability in evaluating alternative forms of financing.)

Now, let's get better acquainted with the basic nature of the major adjustable mortgage programs.

ADJUSTABLE MORTGAGE LOAN (AML)

Federally chartered savings and loan associations are authorized to make AMLs. AMLs replace the variable rate mortgage (VRM) and the renegotiated rate mortgage (RRM) (see Chapter 9), both of which were phased out in August 1981 by the Federal Home Loan Bank Board. The VRM and RRM were stopped because their restrictions on the frequency and amount of interest-rate adjustments made them unpopular with lenders.

In contrast, the AML provides lenders with a wide range of flexibility. There is no limit on the frequency or amount of adjustments to interest rates, as long as the borrower is given 30–45 days' notice. This adjustment can occur by lengthening the loan term up to forty years, by changing the amount of monthly payments, by changing the principal amount, or by a combination of these factors. Other features of the AML include no prepayment penalty, and increases in interest rates are optional at the lender's discretion, but decreases are mandatory.

There is a very interesting feature about AMLs: Although the law does not limit the frequency or amount of adjustments, you may *contractually limit* these terms! Competition in your local lending market may give you some bargaining power and improve your leverage in negotiating periods of adjustment. Don't be timid! If you are, ask your real estate professional or attorney for help.

AVAILABLE INDICES

Changes in the interest rate cannot be determined by the whim of the lender. Rates of change must be linked to some interest-rate index that is readily verifiable by the borrower, and not within the lender's control. The following are four acceptable indices:
  (1) the monthly average yield on U.S. Treasury securities maturing in one, two, three, or five years;

(2) the monthly average yield on three- or six-month U.S. Treasury bills;

(3) the Federal Home Loan Bank Board's (FHLBB) Average Cost
of Funds Index for particular districts;

(4) the FHLBB's index of national average mortgage rates for
purchases of existing homes.

If you expect inflation to slow down, it would be best to pick the
six-month index. If you expect inflation to speed up again, pick the
average mortgage rate charged by all lenders.

ADJUSTABLE RATE MORTGAGE (ARM)

Chartered national banks call their version of the adjustable
mortgage the adjustable rate mortgage (ARM). The ARM was created by legislation in late March 1981. One notable feature of the
ARM is that interest rate adjustments cannot exceed 1 percent
every six months, and any one adjustment cannot exceed 5 percent.

Besides offering a thirty-year maximum loan, regulations also
require that changes in the interest rate MUST be linked to one of
three indices: 1) the monthly average yield on six-month U.S. Treasury Bills; 2) the monthly average yield on three-year U.S. Treasury securities; and 3) the monthly average mortgage rate charged
by all lenders, as published in the Federal Home Loan Bank Board
Journal.

GRADUATED PAYMENT MORTGAGE (GPM)

The graduated payment mortgage (GPM) is the most prominent
variant of the flexible payment plan mortgages (discussed in Chapter 9). Like a conventional loan, the GPM has a fixed interest rate.
Unlike a conventional loan, GPMs start out with lower monthly
payments, and normally increase at 7½ percent each year for five
years. After five years, the borrower "graduates" to the big time,
and pays off the remaining principal at a fixed rate sufficient to
amortize the balance in twenty-five years.

NEGATIVE AMORTIZATION

Note that in the first few years, monthly payments may be too low
to meet the interest payment, let alone apply to the principal bal-

ance. Any unpaid interest will be added to the outstanding principal balance—resulting in a "negative amortization" situation. This is corrected upon graduation, when payments are recalculated to achieve amortization. Consequently, the last twenty-five years of the loan will have higher payments than a similar conventional loan.

The trade-off for these higher deferred costs is that you can buy a home sooner in life, qualifying for a larger loan. For young home buyers, with future salary increases very likely, the GPM is a very helpful first step in the housing market.

PLEDGED ACCOUNT MORTGAGE (PAM)

The pledged account mortgage (PAM) is a special form of the GPM. Recall that a GPM often results in some unpaid interest in early years, due to the reduced monthly payments.

A PAM remedies this problem by having the borrower pledge a savings account to meet any unpaid interest. Deductions from this savings account solve the problem that negative amortization causes in some states that prohibit charging interest on interest owed.

GRADUATED PAYMENT ADJUSTABLE MORTGAGE LOAN (GPAML)

The GPAML combines the major features of the GPM and the AML. Like the GPM, it features low payments in the first few years of the loan (usually five years). After this initial "graduation period" of five years, the GPAML operates exactly as an AML. Review the AML to see what regulations regarding the frequency and magnitude of rate adjustments and choice of index also apply to GPAMLs.

Like a GPM, the initial years of the loan can result in negative amortization. Unlike the AML, within ten years of the closing date, and at least every five years thereafter, the payment must be adjusted to a level sufficient to amortize the remaining balance. The size of the lower initial monthly payments and the number of years in the graduation period (up to ten years by law) are items you can and should negotiate with lenders.

WRAP-AROUND MORTGAGES (WRAP)

The wrap-around mortgage (WRAP) is a variation of the basic assumption. The new financing wraps around the old, and puts two loans in one package. WRAPs are sometimes also called "blended mortgages" or "blends."

Suppose the seller has an existing loan at 9 percent, with monthly payments of $289 and a remaining term of twenty-five years. The loan balance is $30,000. The seller wants $50,000 for the home, but all the cash you have is $5,000 to put down. What can you do?

You might ask the seller to loan you the $15,000 so you can execute a second mortgage (or second deed of trust) in favor of the seller. (Chapter 12 explains assumptions and second mortgages.) If the seller rejects this idea, because he wants to use the equity for other purposes, you still have a chance to structure favorable financing for yourself! Approach the holder of the $30,000 mortgage note, and ask if the holder would consider offering you a WRAP or "blend" mortgage.

You could suggest that you make a $5,000 down payment to the seller's lender (the note holder). You could also suggest that you assume the $30,000 loan balance at 9 percent, with monthly payments of $289, and the lender loans you $15,000 at the going market rate of 14 percent for twenty-five years, with monthly payments of $180.57. You would make total monthly payments of $469.57 on a total loan of $45,000. The interest rate that the lender receives is a "blended" rate of about 11¾ percent. (A check of the mortgage amortization tables shows a $45,000 loan at 11¾ percent for twenty-five years requires monthly payments of $465.66 to amortize.)

BENEFITS OF WRAPS

Everyone benefits from a wrap-around mortgage. The buyer gets a $45,000 loan at a blended rate of 11¾ percent, while the going market rate is 14 percent. The seller can walk away from the transaction with $20,000 equity in his or her pocket. The lender has made a new loan at a blended higher rate of interest.

Now that you understand how WRAPs work, consider the following tips if you contemplate using wrap-around financing. First, if the original lender will not participate in a WRAP, go to *another* lender. You don't have to do business with the holder of the seller's note and mortgage. Second, remember that the original loan must be assumable and contain no "due-on-sale" clause (see Chapter 19). If you and the seller are trying to work out a wrap-around or assumption without the lender's consent, and despite a non-assumption clause, you will wind up with a big legal headache! Get competent advice if you have any doubts.

GROWING EQUITY MORTGAGE (GEM)

One of the most popular new mortgages is the growing equity mortgage (GEM), also called the accelerated principal reduction mortgage (APRM) by Fannie Mae.

With the GEM/APRM the borrower's *monthly payments* are adjusted periodically to compensate the lender for inflation. The extra or incremental payment is applied directly to the principal, thus reducing the loan balance and payoff term in years.

Let's examine a sample GEM to see how it works. Assume the loan is a $60,000, thirty-year GEM loan at 13 percent. The adjustment period will be annual and the adjustment factor will be equal to the annual rate of inflation as measured by the Consumer Price Index (CPI). To simplify matters, let us assume that the adjustment factor rises at a constant rate of 7 percent each year.

On page 108 is a loan summary for our sample GEM/APRM and for a conventional fixed-rate mortgage loan with the same terms.

A comparison of the GEM/APRM and the conventional loan reveals that beginning in the second year the monthly payments are higher for the GEM/APRM. By the tenth year GEM monthly payments are $1,220.22 versus the constant $663.72 called for to amortize the conventional loan. Should these higher monthly payments scare you off? Not really! As long as your income keeps pace with the adjustment factor (CPI-measured inflation) your payments are no increased burden. You pay less total interest under the GEM/APRM, due to the accelerated reduction of the principal. Compare the tenth year. The GEM borrower still owes $10,216.96; but the conventional borrower owes $56,651.88! The GEM/APRM borrower obviously has built up more equity at a faster rate. The GEM/APRM loan is paid off completely by the ninth month of the eleventh year, but the conventional loan is not fully paid off until the end of thirty years.

Many salespeople, lenders, and brokers are hyping the GEM as the loan for today, because it offers something for everyone. The borrower receives the benefit of faster equity build-up through the accelerated reduction of principal and a shorter mortgage life.

Lenders are protected from inflation and will be able to invest the additional payment amounts at newer and higher rates of return in inflationary economic environments. The shorter loan term with a faster payoff also appeals to lenders.

$60,000 Loan at 13% for 30 Years

	GEM/APRM				Conventional Loan		
Year	Monthly Payment	Ending Balance	Total Interest Paid	Year	Monthly Payment	Ending Balance	Total Interest Paid
1	$ 663.72	$59,825.19	$ 7,789.83	1	$ 663.72	$59,825.19	$ 7,789.83
2	710.18	$59,034.28	$15,521.08	2	663.72	$59,626.25	$15,555.53
3	759.89	$57,500.79	$23,106.30	3	663.72	$59,399.85	$23,293.76
4	813.09	$55,077.87	$30,440.40	4	663.72	$59,142.21	$31,000.75
5	870.00	$51,595.32	$37,397.87	5	663.72	$58,848.99	$38,672.18
6	930.90	$46,856.11	$43,829.47	6	663.72	$58,515.31	$46,303.13
7	996.06	$40,632.46	$49,558.59	7	663.72	$58,135.56	$53,888.02
8	1,065.79	$32,661.35	$54,376.95	8	663.72	$57,703.40	$61,420.49
9	1,140.39	$22,639.40	$58,039.72	9	663.72	$57,211.58	$68,893.31
10	1,220.22	$10,216.96	$60,259.95	10	663.72	$56,651.88	$76,298.25
11*	1,305.64	$ .00	$60,778.10	11	663.72	$56,014.93	$83,625.93

*GEM/APRM loan is paid off in the 9th month of the 11th year with a final monthly payment of $290.02.
GEM software and data courtesy of Bogdan Kaczmarek.

THE GEM IS NO JEWEL

Personally, I'm not a big fan of GEMs because they do little, if anything, new for the borrower.

First of all, GEMs do nothing to solve the affordability issue. The income needed to qualify for a GEM/APRM is the same as that required for conventional loans or AMLs. Initial monthly payments are the same as those for conventional loans. Because GEMs are paid off sooner than other loans, advocates suggest that lenders could offer GEMs at a 1–2 percent discount in interest rates. There is little evidence of this occurring, but even if it should occur such a reduction would have only a small impact on the affordability issue.

Second, although the argument that "at least with a GEM/APRM your extra payments go into your own pocket by reducing the loan balance" is true, the same statement is also true if you can prepay principal on your conventional loan! These prepayments on conventional loans are at *your* option, and you can specify the amount you wish to prepay, as opposed to having the lender mandate the amount as happens under GEMs. You can build up as much or more equity as the GEM with a conventional loan, but not with AMLs or ARMs.

THE YUPPIE MORTGAGE

The "Yuppie" mortgage, also called the rapid-amortizing mortgage (RAM), is an exciting concept in home financing. It allows the borrower to make biweekly payments, instead of the normal monthly payments. By making payments every fourteen days, the borrower can build up equity faster, pay off the loan sooner, and reduce the net interest paid over the life of the loan when compared to the traditional thirty-year loan.

For purposes of illustration, let's compare a thirty-year conventional loan for $50,000 at 12 percent with a RAM mortgage of $50,000 at 12 percent. Monthly payments of principal and interest on the conventional loan would be $514.31. With a Yuppie mortgage, you divide the monthly payment of $514.31 in half, and pay $257.16 every two weeks.

Paying every two weeks can make an incredible difference. The Yuppie mortgage is paid off in 18.8 years versus thirty years for the conventional loan. Total interest paid over a thirty-year term would be $135,138.82, versus a total of $75,928.17 under the RAM loan. It could save you $59,210.65 in interest.

I strongly suggest that you investigate the possibility of acquiring a Yuppie mortgage in your area; as an alternative, you can implement a prepayment strategy as outlined in Chapter 18.

WHICH LOAN IS BEST FOR ME?

The smorgasbord of financing presented in this chapter may overwhelm you initially. You'll find this book to be an invaluable aid when you apply for your own home loan, and a careful re-reading of this chapter will be most helpful.

Allow me to offer my perspective on the question, "Which loan should I get?"

If you are seeking a loan from an *institutional* lender, and qualifying is *not* a problem, your best choice is the traditional fixed-rate loan (conventional, FHA, or VA).

Why? Because 1) fixed-rate loans put all the risks of inflation on the lender; 2) constant monthly payments make your budgeting process easier; 3) if interest rates drop you can refinance the loan at lower rates—but if interest rates rise the lender cannot make you pay more; and 4) you may prepay principal, should you choose to do so. Chapters 9, 10, and 11 thoroughly discuss these fixed-rate loans.

If you are seeking a loan from an institutional lender, but you are having *trouble qualifying*, try the SAM (Chapter 9) or GPM to solve your affordability crisis.

17
What about Condominiums and Co-ops?

When you buy a condominium, you buy your dwelling unit or apartment, and take title to the unit in its entirety. You also acquire an undivided tenancy in common interest in the shared areas of the development, such as the clubhouse, lawn, stairways, etc. Although the condominium concept has been around for twenty-five years, the condo craze really took hold in the late 1970s.

THE CONDO MARKET FROM 1975–1985

What makes condos so popular? Several factors. Many homeowners have always dreamed of having a second place near the ocean, in the mountains, or in ritzy neighborhoods. They can make those dreams come true by purchasing a $70,000 condo in a plush area laced with $300,000 homes. Condos offer amenities, such as saunas, pools, spas, tennis courts, clubhouses, landscaping, and even golf courses. Owners are relieved of maintenance tasks, such as mowing the lawn or shoveling snow.

For first-time buyers, a condominium represents a viable alternative to a single-family home that they may not be able to afford in a period of rapidly rising inflation and escalating home prices. The condo buyer can enjoy the same tax advantages and financial leverage as the home buyer.

Condos are marketed to first-time buyers as a way to take that first step on the ladder of opportunity in the housing game. The strategy is this: buy a condo, hold it a few years while inflation and market forces drive its value up, then sell the condo and use the equity (profit) as a down payment on a house.

Sound like a workable strategy? Maybe! The two underlying assumptions must be correct. First, prices must continue to rise, and second, when you desire to sell there must be a buyer.

By 1982, it became apparent to condo owners that market forces had drastically changed. On the supply side, a glut of units occurred virtually everywhere. Not only did new construction add to the supply, but so did the staggering amount of apartment conversions. The major factors that contributed to slackening demand included high interest rates, little if any price appreciation, and a very soft resale market.

CONDO HEADACHES

There are many factors that a potential condo buyer must be aware of before making a well-informed decision. All condo owners become members of the Condominium Homeowners Association. The purpose of the association is to manage and regulate affairs relating to the common property. The written body of rules and regulations of the association are often called "by-laws" or "articles of association."

You should *always* examine the bylaws before purchasing a condo. Look for restrictions regarding children, pets, use of the clubhouse, pool, tennis courts, etc.

As a member of the association, you will pay a monthly fee or assessment to cover management and maintenance expenses.

WHAT TO WATCH FOR

Here are some things to watch for, and some questions to consider, regarding the financial aspects of the association.

Who are the directors and officers of the association? Who are the managers? What is the quality of their work? Are they professionals, or just some residents who have little financial or management expertise? What about reserve funds or contingency funds? If the development needs a new roof or the driveway and parking areas need to be resurfaced, are there available funds, or will the owners need to pay a special assessment fee for these items? If professional management is retained, who are they? Are they connected with the builder or developer? If so, do they have a "sweetheart" contract that locks the association into a long-term deal? Are monthly fees similar to fees charged by comparable developments in the same locale?

Are the financial statements and books accurate and timely? Are past expenses in line with past budgets? Does the association carry adequate liability insurance in case of personal injury arising from activities in the common areas?

If answers, records, and bylaws are not immediately available for your inspection, you should not consider the project.

KIDDIE CONDOS

Lack of available housing in some college towns and areas has given birth to the college or "kiddie" condo market. Parents buy a condo and rent it to their children. The parents get the tax advantages of depreciation and interest expenses. After the children graduate, the parents attempt to sell the condo, hopefully at a profit. A word of caution is in order here. Resale markets for college condos are more volatile than the general condo market, and many parents have been burned. If parents must buy their children some type of housing, why not buy a single-family home? The chances for appreciation and resale are better with a house than a condo.

A FINAL WORD ON CONDOS

Well-managed condominium projects can be a joy to live in, providing amenities and a lifestyle about which homeowners can only dream. Poorly managed projects can give owners headaches and drain their savings accounts.

One final word of advice: If you do buy a condo, do NOT allow yourself to be elected or appointed to serve as a director or officer of the association without realizing that you can be *personally* sued for a variety of errors or omissions!

CO-OPERATIVE HOUSING

Co-operative apartments, or "co-ops," may seem like condominiums, but they are very different in a legal sense. Unlike the condo, the purchaser does NOT take title to or own his dwelling unit. All units and common areas are owned by the co-operative corporation or trust. Each purchaser receives a share of stock in the corporation, and also a lease granting the right to occupy a specific dwelling unit.

The co-op corporation usually finances the entire complex by obtaining a blanket mortgage for the project. Shareholders pay off the mortgage in pro-rated unit-share amounts. Shareholders also pay monthly assessments for management and maintenance.

Because the co-op dweller cannot directly deduct mortgage interest and property taxes for income tax purposes, co-ops are not as popular as condos. Proposed legislation in various states would alter some features of the co-op to make it more attractive to purchasers. Hybrid forms of the co-op, such as the "co-opdominium," are under consideration by some legislatures.

Due to the legal and financial complications inherent in the co-op from state to state, you should see a good real estate attorney before purchasing.

18
Amortization Schedules and Prepayment Strategy

This chapter contains some exciting information that could save you $50,000 or more in loan payments, and help you to pay off your loan in half the time! To implement the strategy that I recommend, it is necessary to have an understanding of how amortization schedules work.

AMORTIZATION SCHEDULE

An amortization schedule is a timetable for periodic payments (usually monthly), which will settle a debt sometime in the future. Home loans are typically due thirty years after they are made. The payments include money applied towards reducing the loan balance (the principal), and money applied as interest on the loan.

When you borrow money to buy a home, the lender will provide you with an amortization schedule at closing. Suppose you borrow $50,000 at 13 percent for thirty years. An amortization schedule for this loan is shown on page 116.

Take a minute to understand this schedule—360 equal monthly payments of $553.10 are necessary to amortize this loan. Note that your first monthly payment consists of $541.67 in interest and only $11.43 applied towards reducing the $50,000 principal. The schedule shows that after the first payment the principal is reduced to a balance of $49,988.57 (calculated by subtracting $11.43 from $50,000).

PRINCIPAL = $50,000.00
INTEREST RATE = 0.13000
LOAN LIFE IS 30 YEARS   **MONTHLY PAYMENT = $553.10**

NUM	INTEREST	PRIN. PAY	PRIN. BAL	INTEREST PAID TO DATE
1	$ 541.67	$ 11.43	$ 49988.57	$ 541.67
2	$ 541.54	$ 11.56	$ 49977.01	$ 1083.21
3	$ 541.42	$ 11.68	$ 49965.33	$ 1624.63
4	$ 541.29	$ 11.81	$ 49953.52	$ 2165.92
5	$ 541.16	$ 11.94	$ 49941.58	$ 2707.08
6	$ 541.03	$ 12.07	$ 49929.52	$ 3248.12
7	$ 540.90	$ 12.20	$ 49917.32	$ 3789.02
8	$ 540.77	$ 12.33	$ 49904.99	$ 4329.79
9	$ 540.64	$ 12.46	$ 49892.53	$ 4870.43
10	$ 540.50	$ 12.60	$ 49879.93	$ 5410.93
11	$ 540.37	$ 12.73	$ 49867.20	$ 5951.29
12	$ 540.23	$ 12.87	$ 49854.33	$ 6491.52
13	$ 540.09	$ 13.01	$ 49841.31	$ 7031.61
14	$ 539.95	$ 13.15	$ 49828.16	$ 7571.56
15	$ 539.81	$ 13.29	$ 49814.87	$ 8111.36
16	$ 539.66	$ 13.44	$ 49801.43	$ 8651.03
17	$ 539.52	$ 13.58	$ 49787.84	$ 9190.54
18	$ 539.37	$ 13.73	$ 49774.11	$ 9729.91
19	$ 539.22	$ 13.88	$ 49760.23	$ 10269.13
20	$ 539.07	$ 14.03	$ 49746.20	$ 10808.20
21	$ 538.92	$ 14.18	$ 49732.02	$ 11347.11
22	$ 538.76	$ 14.34	$ 49717.68	$ 11885.88
23	$ 538.61	$ 14.49	$ 49703.19	$ 12424.49
24	$ 538.45	$ 14.65	$ 49688.54	$ 12962.94

(Payments #25 through #336 are not reprinted here.)

NUM	INTEREST	PRIN. PAY	PRIN. BAL	INTEREST PAID TO DATE
337	$ 126.03	$ 427.07	$ 11206.90	$147601.52
338	$ 121.41	$ 431.69	$ 10775.21	$147722.92
339	$ 116.73	$ 436.37	$ 10338.84	$147839.66
340	$ 112.00	$ 441.10	$ 9897.74	$147951.66
341	$ 107.23	$ 445.87	$ 9451.87	$148058.88
342	$ 102.40	$ 450.70	$ 9001.16	$148161.28
343	$ 97.51	$ 455.59	$ 8545.58	$148258.79
344	$ 92.58	$ 460.52	$ 8085.05	$148351.37
345	$ 87.59	$ 465.51	$ 7619.54	$148438.96
346	$ 82.55	$ 470.55	$ 7148.99	$148521.50
347	$ 77.45	$ 475.65	$ 6673.33	$148598.95
348	$ 72.29	$ 480.81	$ 6192.53	$148671.24
349	$ 67.09	$ 486.01	$ 5706.51	$148738.33
350	$ 61.82	$ 491.28	$ 5215.24	$148800.15
351	$ 56.50	$ 496.60	$ 4718.63	$148856.65
352	$ 51.12	$ 501.98	$ 4216.65	$148907.77
353	$ 45.68	$ 507.42	$ 3709.23	$148953.45
354	$ 40.18	$ 512.92	$ 3196.32	$148993.63
355	$ 34.63	$ 518.47	$ 2677.84	$149028.26
356	$ 29.01	$ 524.09	$ 2153.75	$149057.27
357	$ 23.33	$ 529.77	$ 1623.99	$149080.60
358	$ 17.59	$ 535.51	$ 1088.48	$149098.19
359	$ 11.79	$ 541.31	$ 547.17	$149109.99
360	$ 5.93	$ 547.17	$ 0.00	$149115.91

PREPAYING THE PRINCIPAL BALANCE

In some cases, you may wish to pay off some or all of the principal balance early. Why? One good reason might be that you sell your home. Another reason might be to save on interest charges by reducing the principal balance at an accelerated rate.

Can you prepay principal? Yes, if the lender agrees to it in the promissory note. Some lenders charge a prepayment fee. Most of them insist that if principal is going to be prepaid, the amounts must exactly equal the sum listed in the amortization schedule.

For example, return to the amortization schedule on page 116. Let's suppose you wish to prepay principal on your very first monthly payment. You must first pay the $553.10 installment. Any amount paid above this figure will reduce the principal. If you elect to pay an extra $100, your remaining principal balance would drop from $49,988.57 to $49,888.57. But notice that this new balance does *not* show up anywhere on the schedule! The amortization schedule is now useless, and the lender would have to generate a completely new schedule based upon the new principal balance and 359 months. (And you would have to pay $10–$50 for this new paperwork!)

You can avoid this extra expense by prepaying an amount that will jibe exactly with the schedule. Utilizing the example to prepay $100, the following is an effective methodology to avoid prepayment fees or penalties.

Look at the column "Principal Payment," beginning with the second payment, which is $11.56. Add to this the next principal payment of $11.68, which totals $23.24. Keep adding the principal payments until you reach a total figure *close* to $100. If you add the second through the ninth principal payments, the amount totals $96.05.

If you prepaid $96.05, your next payment due would be the tenth one on the schedule. You obviously save some interest expenses by accelerating the reduction of the principal. By prepaying this exact amount ($96.05) that jibes with the amortization schedule, you also avoid any prepayment fees.

YOUR SAVINGS ARE SUBSTANTIAL

Would *you* spend the extra $96.05 to save $4,328.75 (the total interest for the second through ninth payments) in future interest payments? Sure you would! Remember, should you make payments for the full thirty years, you're going to pay a total of $149,115.91 in just *interest*—plus the $50,000 borrowed principal. That's a lot of money, and you need all the help you can get!

Why not just get a fifteen-year "jumbo mortgage" for $50,000 at 13 percent? There are two good reasons to select the prepayment strategy. First of all, you would have larger monthly payments of $632.62 on the fifteen-year loan, compared to the $553.10 payment on the thirty-year loan. This extra monthly amount of $79.52 means that you must earn an extra $3,816.96 per year in order to *qualify* for the fifteen-year loan.

Second, the jumbo loan *requires* you to make the larger, fixed monthly payments every month. It is better to prepay principal on a thirty-year loan in various extra amounts of your choice, and only in the months that you choose. You may prefer spending that extra amount on something else and resume your prepayment strategy the next month.

Not only will this prepayment strategy work for you as you begin payments on your new home, but it will also work well for your friends who have been paying off their mortgages for years. Explain this strategy to them and they will be very grateful.

19
What You Should Know about Mortgages

The word "mortgage" conjures up thoughts of signing your life away for thirty years, and a document full of difficult language.

Mortgages are referred to in some states as deeds of trust, or first deeds. A mortgage is simply the giving of an interest in real property for the purpose of securing a debt or obligation. In legal terminology, your buildings are considered improvements upon the real property.

The buyer is the borrower. The borrower is called the mortgagor; the lender is the mortgagee.

A mortgage consists of basically two separate instruments, although they may be combined in a single form. These instruments are:

(1) **The Promissory Note:**
The borrower acknowledges his debt to the lender and promises to pay the debt in the manner described (like monthly payments of X dollars for 30 years). The promissory note is in effect a legal I.O.U.

(2) **The Mortgage:**
In effect, this is a specific type of security agreement, with the land and all improvements serving as the collateral. The borrower gives an interest in his real property to the lender, until his I.O.U. is paid.

The mortgage contains several clauses that deserve our attention and analysis.

First, consider the "prepayment clause." This clause allows the borrower to pay off his loan balance at any time before the due date, without paying unaccrued interest. The borrower should insist that there be no penalty fees for an early repayment of the total loan. The lender may charge you some administrative fees of sorts, but make sure that this is defined in the agreement.

Why worry about this clause? Because you might want to sell your home before the loan term expires, or you might want to pay off the balance earlier than the amortized payment schedule calls for, to save yourself interest.

Also, suppose your loan rate is 11½ percent, and a couple of years from now the interest rate drops to 9 percent. You might want to refinance your loan at this cheaper rate. Don't plan on any big drops in the interest rate, but be in a position to do something to benefit yourself should this miraculous event occur!

The second clause is called the "non-assumption" clause. It typically prohibits the assumption of your loan by another person. Sometimes it allows assumptions, but only at the approval and discretion of the lender.

How does this affect you? Should you later decide to sell your home, your buyer may insist upon an assumption as part of the financing conditions. FHA and VA loans are assumable. Conventional loans made in recent years are not. Why? Because the clause has become very popular with lenders since about 1970. If one lender has it in your area, the odds are good that they all do. You could ask that the clause be removed, but I doubt if you would succeed. It really affects your future resale in a small way, when one considers the other avenues of financing available.

It's easy to denounce the lenders as a bloodthirsty lot, but this practice really does not differ from other practices of adjusting wages, prices, or salaries as time marches on. Is your paycheck the same as when interest rates were 6 percent? Are prices of the goods and services you buy the same? No! And neither is the cost of borrowed money.

Sample Mortgage Form

Box 134

MORTGAGE

TO

CHESTERFIELD FEDERAL
**SAVINGS AND LOAN ASSOCIATION
OF CHICAGO**

10801 SOUTH WESTERN AVENUE

LOAN NO.

RECORDER'S STAMP:

142-3 79-2M

MORTGAGE

THIS INDENTURE WITNESSETH: That the undersigned,

of the   of   County of   State of Illinois,

hereinafter referred to as the Mortgagor, does hereby Mortgage and Warrant to

Chesterfield Federal Savings and Loan Association of Chicago

a corporation organized and existing under the laws of the United States, hereinafter referred to as the Mortgagee, the following real estate, situated in the County of Cook, in the State of Illinois, to wit:

TOGETHER with all the buildings and improvements now or hereafter erected thereon, including all gas and electric fixtures, including screens, window shades, storm doors and windows, attached floor coverings, in-a-door beds, awnings, stoves and water heaters, plumbing apparatus, motors, boilers, furnaces, ranges, refrigerators, and all apparatus and fixtures of every kind, whether used for the purpose of supplying or distributing heat, refrigeration, light, water, air, power or otherwise, now in or which hereafter may be placed in any building or improvement now or hereafter upon said property (all of which are declared to be a part of said real estate, whether physically attached thereto or not); together with all easements and rents, issues and profits thereof which are hereby assigned, transferred and set over unto the Mortgagee, whether now due or which may hereafter become due under or by virtue of any lease whether written or verbal, or any agreement for the use or occupancy of said property, or any part or parts thereof, which may have been heretofore, or may be hereafter made or agreed to, or which may be made and agreed to by the Mortgagee under the power herein granted to it; it being the intention hereby to establish an absolute transfer and assignment to the Mortgagee of all such leases and agreements and all the avails thereunder, together with the right on the part of the Mortgagee to collect all of said avails, rents, issues and profits arising or accruing at any time hereafter and all now due or that may hereafter become due under each and every of the leases or agreements existing or to hereafter exist for said premises, and to use such measures, legal or equitable, as in its discretion may be deemed proper or necessary to enforce the payment or security of said avails, rents, issues and profits, or to secure and maintain possession of said premises, or any portion thereof, and to fill any and all vacancies and to rent, lease or let any portion of said premises to any party or parties, at its discretion, with power to use and apply said avails, issues and profits to the payment of any expenses, care and management of said premises, including taxes and assessments, and to the payment of any indebtedness secured hereby or incurred hereunder.

TO HAVE AND TO HOLD the said property, with said appurtenances, apparatus and fixtures, unto said Mortgagee forever, for the uses herein set forth, free from all rights and benefits under the Homestead Exemption Laws of the State of Illinois, which said rights and benefits the said Mortgagor does hereby release and waive.

TO SECURE: (1) the payment of a certain indebtedness from the Mortgagor to the Mortgagee in the principal sum of

DOLLARS ($), together with interest thereon as provided by a note of even date herewith made by the Mortgagor in favor of the Mortgagee evidencing said indebtedness, said principal and interest being payable as provided in said note until the entire sum is paid.

(2) Any additional advances made by the Mortgagee to the Mortgagor, or his successors in title, for any purpose, at any time prior to the cancellation of this mortgage, provided that this mortgage shall not at any time secure more than

DOLLARS ($), together with interest thereon, plus any advances necessary for the protection and/or enforcement of the lien of this mortgage.

THE MORTGAGOR COVENANTS:

(1) To either pay immediately when due and payable all general taxes, special assessments and other taxes levied or assessed upon said property or any part thereof and to promptly deliver receipts therefor to the Mortgagee upon demand; or pay such items in accordance with the terms of the note of even date herewith; (2) To keep the improvements now or hereafter upon said premises insured against damage by fire, windstorm and such other hazards as the Mortgagee may require to be insured against, until said indebtedness is fully paid, or in case of foreclosure, until expiration of the period of redemption, for the full insurable value thereof, in such companies and by agencies to be approved by Mortgagee and in such form as shall be satisfactory to the Mortgagee; such insurance policies shall remain with the Mortgagee during said period or periods, and contain the usual clause making them payable to the Mortgagee, and in case of foreclosure sale payable to the owner of the certificate of sale; and in case of loss, the Mortgagee is authorized to adjust, collect and compromise, in its discretion, all claims under such policies, and the Mortgagor agrees to sign, upon demand, all receipts, vouchers and releases required of him by the insurance companies; and the Mortgagee is authorized to apply the proceeds of any insurance claim upon the indebtedness hereby secured in its discretion, but monthly payments shall continue until said indebtedness is paid in full; (3) Not to commit or suffer any waste of said property, and to maintain the same in good condition and repair; (4) To promptly pay all bills for such repairs and all other expenses incident to the ownership of said property in order that no lien of mechanics or materialmen shall attach to said property; (5) Not to suffer or permit any unlawful use of or any nuisance to exist upon said property; (6) Not to diminish or impair the value of said property or the security intended to be effected by virtue of this mortgage by any act or omission to act; (7) To appear in and defend any proceeding which in the opinion of the Mortgagee affects its security hereunder, and to pay all costs, expenses and attorney's fees incurred or paid by the Mortgagee in any proceedings in which it may be made a party defendant by reason of this mortgage; (8) Not to suffer or permit without the written permission or consent of the Mortgagee being first had and obtained (a) any use of said property for a purpose other than that for which the same is now used; (b) any alterations, additions to, demolition or removal of any of the improvements, apparatus, fixtures or equipment now or hereafter upon said property; (c) a purchase upon conditional sale, lease or agreement under which title is reserved in the vendor, of any apparatus, fixtures or equipment to be placed in or upon any building or improvement upon said property; (d) a sale, assignment or transfer of any right, title or interest in and to said property or any portion thereof, or any of the improvements, apparatus, fixtures or equipment which may be found in or upon said property, and

THE MORTGAGOR FURTHER COVENANTS:

(1) That in case of his failure to perform any of his covenants herein, the Mortgagee may do on his behalf everything so covenanted; that said Mortgagee may also do any act it may deem necessary to protect the lien of this mortgage; and that he will immediately repay any moneys paid or disbursed by the Mortgagee for any of the above purposes, and such moneys together with interest thereon at the highest rate for which it is then lawful to contract shall become so much additional indebtedness secured by this mortgage and may be included in any decree foreclosing this mortgage and be paid out of the rents or proceeds of the sale of said premises, if not otherwise paid by him; that it shall not be obligatory upon the Mortgagee to inquire into the validity of any lien, encumbrance or claim in advancing moneys in that behalf as above authorized, but nothing herein contained shall be construed as requiring the Mortgagee to advance any moneys for any purpose nor to do any act hereunder; that the Mortgagee shall not incur personal liability because of anything it may do or omit to do hereunder;

(2) That it is the intent hereof to secure payment of said Note whether the entire amount shall have been advanced to the Mortgagor at the date hereof or at a later date, or having been advanced, shall have been repaid in part and further advances made at a later date, which advances shall in no event operate to make the principal sum of the indebtedness greater than the amount named in said Note plus any amount or amounts that may be added to the mortgage indebtedness under the terms hereof;

(3) That if the Mortgagor shall apply for and obtain a policy of insurance on his life, and disability insurance for loss of time by accidental injury or sickness, or either such contract, under which the Mortgagee is beneficiary or assignee of the interest of the beneficiary, the Mortgagee has the right to advance the first annual premium and add such payment to the unpaid balance of the loan, as of the then current month, and it shall become additional indebtedness secured by the mortgage. It is further understood that if the Mortgagee advances said insurance premium, the Mortgagor agrees to pay each month, in addition to the principal and interest installments required herein, a sum equivalent to one-twelfth of the annual premium, which is to be placed in the Tax and Insurance Account in accordance with the terms and provisions contained therein.

(4) That in the event the ownership of said property or any part thereof becomes vested in a person other than the Mortgagor, the Mortgagee may, without notice to the Mortgagor, deal with such successor or successors in interest with reference to this mortgage and the debt hereby secured in the same manner as with the Mortgagor, and may forebear to sue or may extend time for payment of the debt secured hereby without discharging or in any way affecting the liability of the Mortgagor hereunder or upon the debt hereby secured;

(5) That time is of the essence hereof and if default be made in performance of any covenant herein contained or in making any payment under said Note or any extension or renewal thereof, or if proceedings be instituted to enforce any other lien or charge upon any of said property, or upon the filing of a proceeding in bankruptcy by or against the Mortgagor, or if the Mortgagor shall make an assignment for the benefit of his creditors or if his property be placed under control of or in custody of any court, or if the Mortgagor abandon any of said property, then and in any of said events, the Mortgagee is hereby authorized and empowered, at its option, and without effecting the lien hereby created or the priority of said lien or any right of the Mortgagee hereunder, to declare, without notice, all sums secured hereby immediately due and payable, whether or not such default be remedied by the Mortgagor, and apply toward the payment of said mortgage indebtedness any indebtedness of the Mortgagee to the Mortgagor, and said Mortgagee may also immediately proceed to foreclose this mortgage;

(6) That upon the commencement of any foreclosure proceeding hereunder, the court in which such bill is filed may, at any time, either before or after sale, and without notice to the Mortgagor or any party claiming under him and without regard to the then value of said premises, or whether the same shall then be occupied by the owner of the equity of redemption as a homestead, appoint a receiver with power to manage and rent and to collect the rents, issues and profits of said premises during the pendency of such foreclosure suit and the statutory period of redemption, and such rents, issues and profits, when collected, may be applied before as well as after the master's sale, towards the payment of the indebtedness, costs, taxes, insurance or other items necessary for the protection and preservation of the property, including the expenses of such receivership; and upon foreclosure and sale of said premises there shall be first paid out of the proceeds of such sale a reasonable sum for attorneys' or solicitors' fees, and also all expenses of advertising, selling and conveying said premises, and all moneys advanced for insurance, taxes or other liens or assessments, outlays for documentary evidence, stenographers' charges, all court costs, master's fees, and costs of procuring or completing an abstract of title or guarantee policy or Torrens Certificate showing the whole title to said premises, and including the foreclosure decree and the Master's Certificate of Sale; then to pay the principal indebtedness whether due and payable by the terms hereof or not, and the interest due thereon up to the time of such sale, rendering the overplus, if any, unto the Mortgagor, and it shall not be the duty of the purchaser to see to the application of the purchase money; and in case of payment of said indebtedness, after the filing of any bill to foreclose this mortgage, and prior to the entry of a decree of sale, a reasonable sum for legal services, rendered to the time of such payment shall be allowed as solicitors' fees, which, together with any sum paid for continuation of abstract, court costs, and stenographers' charges and expenses of such proceeding, shall be additional indebtedness hereby secured;

(7) In case the mortgaged property, or any part thereof, shall be taken by condemnation, the Mortgagee is hereby empowered to collect and receive all compensation which may be paid for any property taken or for damages to any property not taken, and all condemnation money so received shall be forthwith applied by the Mortgagee as it may elect, to the immediate reduction of the indebtedness secured hereby, or to the repair and restoration of any property so damaged;

(8) That each right, power and remedy herein conferred upon the Mortgagee is cumulative of every other right or remedy of the Mortgagee, whether herein or by law conferred, and may be enforced concurrently therewith; that no waiver by the Mortgagee, of performance of any covenant herein or in said obligation contained shall thereafter in any manner affect the right of Mortgagee to require or enforce performance of the same or any other of said covenants; that wherever the context hereof requires, the masculine gender, as used herein, shall include the feminine, and the singular number, as used herein, shall include the plural; that all rights and obligations under this mortgage shall extend to and be binding on the respective heirs, executors, administrators, successors and assigns of the Mortgagor and the Mortgagee.

IN WITNESS WHEREOF, we have hereunto set our hands and seals, this .... day of .... A. D. 19............

....(SEAL)   ....(SEAL)

....(SEAL)   ....(SEAL)

STATE OF ILLINOIS |
COUNTY OF COOK | ss.

I,.., a Notary Public in and for said County, in the State aforesaid, DO HEREBY CERTIFY that ....

personally known to me to be the same person   whose name   subscribed to the foregoing Instrument, appeared before me this day in person, and acknowledged that   signed, sealed and delivered the said Instrument as   free and voluntary act, for the uses and purposes therein set forth, including the release and waiver of the right of homestead.

GIVEN under my hand and Notarial Seal, this .... day of .... A. D. 19............

....
Notary Public

Monthly Mortgage Payment

The following tables show you the monthly payments necessary to amortize (or fully pay) a given loan amount at a given interest rate, for a period of years. The monthly payment is one sum that includes repayment on the principal loan amount, plus interest payment.

Let's work an example together. If you borrow $30,000 at 14 percent for thirty years, what will your monthly payments be?

Look at the following pages, and find 14 percent. Then locate the loan amount—$30,000. The corresponding figure under the thirty-year column is $355.46. That $355.46 is your monthly payment on principal and interest to the lender. These tables do not include monthly charges for taxes and insurance, you learned how to calculate these in the Financing chapters.

O.K., let's try one more, to be *sure* you know how to use these tables. What are the monthly payments for a $43,550 loan at 13 percent for thirty years? First, locate the 13 percent page and thirty-year column.

(1) Find the monthly payment for $40,000 = $442.48
(2) Find the monthly payment for $3,000 =   33.19
(3) Find the monthly payment for $500 =   5.53
(4) Find the monthly payment for $50 =   .55
(5) Total $481.75

Get the idea? If not, go over it again!

YEARLY INTEREST RATE = 8.00%

LOAN LIFE IN YEARS

PRINCIPAL	10	15	20	25	30
			MONTHLY PAYMENTS		
$ 25.00	$ .30	$ .24	$ .21	$ .19	$ .18
$ 50.00	.61	.48	.42	.39	.37
$ 100.00	1.21	.96	.84	.77	.73
$ 200.00	2.43	1.91	1.67	1.54	1.47
$ 300.00	3.64	2.87	2.51	2.32	2.20
$ 400.00	4.85	3.82	3.35	3.09	2.94
$ 500.00	6.07	4.78	4.18	3.86	3.67
$ 1000.00	12.13	9.56	8.36	7.72	7.34
$ 2000.00	24.27	19.11	16.73	15.44	14.68
$ 3000.00	36.40	28.67	25.09	23.15	22.01
$ 4000.00	48.53	38.23	33.46	30.87	29.35
$ 5000.00	60.66	47.78	41.82	38.59	36.69
$ 10000.00	121.33	95.57	83.64	77.18	73.38
$ 15000.00	181.99	143.35	125.47	115.77	110.06
$ 20000.00	242.66	191.13	167.29	154.36	146.75
$ 25000.00	303.32	238.91	209.11	192.95	183.44
$ 30000.00	363.98	286.70	250.93	231.54	220.13
$ 35000.00	424.65	334.48	292.75	270.14	256.82
$ 40000.00	485.31	382.26	334.58	308.73	293.51
$ 45000.00	545.97	430.04	376.40	347.32	330.19
$ 50000.00	606.64	477.83	418.22	385.91	366.88
$ 55000.00	667.30	525.61	460.04	424.50	403.57
$ 60000.00	727.97	573.39	501.86	463.09	440.26
$ 65000.00	788.63	621.17	543.69	501.68	476.95
$ 70000.00	849.29	668.96	585.51	540.27	513.64
$ 75000.00	909.96	716.74	627.33	578.86	550.32
$ 80000.00	970.62	764.52	669.15	617.45	587.01
$ 85000.00	1031.28	812.30	710.97	656.04	623.70
$ 90000.00	1091.95	860.09	752.80	694.63	660.39
$ 95000.00	1152.61	907.87	794.62	733.23	697.08
$100000.00	1213.28	955.65	836.44	771.82	733.76
$125000.00	1516.59	1194.56	1045.55	964.77	917.21
$150000.00	1819.91	1433.48	1254.66	1157.72	1100.65

YEARLY INTEREST RATE = 8.25%

LOAN LIFE IN YEARS

PRINCIPAL	10	15	20	25	30
			MONTHLY PAYMENTS		
$ 25.00	$ .31	$ .24	$ .21	$ .20	$ .19
$ 50.00	.61	.49	.43	.39	.38
$ 100.00	1.23	.97	.85	.79	.75
$ 200.00	2.45	1.94	1.70	1.58	1.50
$ 300.00	3.68	2.91	2.56	2.37	2.25
$ 400.00	4.91	3.88	3.41	3.15	3.01
$ 500.00	6.13	4.85	4.26	3.94	3.76
$ 1000.00	12.27	9.70	8.52	7.88	7.51
$ 2000.00	24.53	19.40	17.04	15.77	15.03
$ 3000.00	36.80	29.10	25.56	23.65	22.54
$ 4000.00	49.06	38.81	34.08	31.54	30.05
$ 5000.00	61.33	48.51	42.60	39.42	37.56
$ 10000.00	122.65	97.01	85.21	78.85	75.13
$ 15000.00	183.98	145.52	127.81	118.27	112.69
$ 20000.00	245.31	194.03	170.41	157.69	150.25
$ 25000.00	306.63	242.54	213.02	197.11	187.82
$ 30000.00	367.96	291.04	255.62	236.54	225.38
$ 35000.00	429.28	339.55	298.22	275.96	262.94
$ 40000.00	490.61	388.06	340.83	315.38	300.51
$ 45000.00	551.94	436.56	383.43	354.80	338.07
$ 50000.00	613.26	485.07	426.03	394.23	375.63
$ 55000.00	674.59	533.58	468.64	433.65	413.20
$ 60000.00	735.92	582.08	511.24	473.07	450.76
$ 65000.00	797.24	630.59	553.84	512.49	488.32
$ 70000.00	858.57	679.10	596.45	551.92	525.89
$ 75000.00	919.89	727.61	639.05	591.34	563.45
$ 80000.00	981.22	776.11	681.65	630.76	601.01
$ 85000.00	1042.55	824.62	724.26	670.18	638.58
$ 90000.00	1103.87	873.13	766.86	709.61	676.14
$ 95000.00	1165.20	921.63	809.46	749.03	713.70
$100000.00	1226.53	970.14	852.07	788.45	751.27
$125000.00	1533.16	1212.68	1065.08	985.56	939.08
$150000.00	1839.79	1455.21	1278.10	1182.68	1126.90

YEARLY INTEREST RATE = 8.50%

LOAN LIFE IN YEARS

MONTHLY PAYMENTS

PRINCIPAL	10	15	20	25	30
$ 25.00	$ .31	$ .25	$ .22	$ .20	$ .19
$ 50.00	$ .62	$ .49	$ .43	$ .40	$ .38
$ 100.00	$ 1.24	$ .98	$ .87	$ .81	$ .77
$ 200.00	$ 2.48	$ 1.97	$ 1.74	$ 1.61	$ 1.54
$ 300.00	$ 3.72	$ 2.95	$ 2.60	$ 2.42	$ 2.31
$ 400.00	$ 4.96	$ 3.94	$ 3.47	$ 3.22	$ 3.08
$ 500.00	$ 6.20	$ 4.92	$ 4.34	$ 4.03	$ 3.84
$ 1000.00	$ 12.40	$ 9.85	$ 8.68	$ 8.05	$ 7.69
$ 2000.00	$ 24.80	$ 19.69	$ 17.36	$ 16.10	$ 15.38
$ 3000.00	$ 37.20	$ 29.54	$ 26.03	$ 24.16	$ 23.07
$ 4000.00	$ 49.59	$ 39.39	$ 34.71	$ 32.21	$ 30.76
$ 5000.00	$ 61.99	$ 49.24	$ 43.39	$ 40.26	$ 38.45
$ 10000.00	$ 123.99	$ 98.47	$ 86.78	$ 80.52	$ 76.89
$ 15000.00	$ 185.98	$ 147.71	$ 130.17	$ 120.78	$ 115.34
$ 20000.00	$ 247.97	$ 196.95	$ 173.56	$ 161.05	$ 153.78
$ 25000.00	$ 309.96	$ 246.18	$ 216.96	$ 201.31	$ 192.23
$ 30000.00	$ 371.96	$ 295.42	$ 260.35	$ 241.57	$ 230.67
$ 35000.00	$ 433.95	$ 344.66	$ 303.74	$ 281.83	$ 269.12
$ 40000.00	$ 495.94	$ 393.90	$ 347.13	$ 322.09	$ 307.57
$ 45000.00	$ 557.94	$ 443.13	$ 390.52	$ 362.35	$ 346.01
$ 50000.00	$ 619.93	$ 492.37	$ 433.91	$ 402.61	$ 384.46
$ 55000.00	$ 681.92	$ 541.61	$ 477.30	$ 442.87	$ 422.90
$ 60000.00	$ 743.91	$ 590.84	$ 520.69	$ 483.14	$ 461.35
$ 65000.00	$ 805.91	$ 640.08	$ 564.09	$ 523.40	$ 499.79
$ 70000.00	$ 867.90	$ 689.32	$ 607.48	$ 563.66	$ 538.24
$ 75000.00	$ 929.89	$ 738.55	$ 650.87	$ 603.92	$ 576.68
$ 80000.00	$ 991.89	$ 787.79	$ 694.26	$ 644.18	$ 615.13
$ 85000.00	$1053.88	$ 837.03	$ 737.65	$ 684.44	$ 653.58
$ 90000.00	$1115.87	$ 886.27	$ 781.04	$ 724.70	$ 692.02
$ 95000.00	$1177.86	$ 935.50	$ 824.43	$ 764.97	$ 730.47
$100000.00	$1239.86	$ 984.74	$ 867.82	$ 805.23	$ 768.91
$125000.00	$1549.82	$1230.92	$1084.78	$1006.53	$ 961.14
$150000.00	$1859.79	$1477.11	$1301.73	$1207.84	$1153.37

YEARLY INTEREST RATE = 8.75%

LOAN LIFE IN YEARS

MONTHLY PAYMENTS

PRINCIPAL	10	15	20	25	30
$ 25.00	$ .31	$ .25	$ .22	$ .21	$ .20
$ 50.00	$ .63	$ .50	$ .44	$ .41	$ .39
$ 100.00	$ 1.25	$ 1.00	$ .88	$ .82	$ .79
$ 200.00	$ 2.51	$ 2.00	$ 1.77	$ 1.64	$ 1.57
$ 300.00	$ 3.76	$ 3.00	$ 2.65	$ 2.47	$ 2.36
$ 400.00	$ 5.01	$ 4.00	$ 3.53	$ 3.29	$ 3.15
$ 500.00	$ 6.27	$ 5.00	$ 4.42	$ 4.11	$ 3.93
$ 1000.00	$ 12.53	$ 9.99	$ 8.84	$ 8.22	$ 7.87
$ 2000.00	$ 25.07	$ 19.99	$ 17.67	$ 16.44	$ 15.73
$ 3000.00	$ 37.60	$ 29.98	$ 26.51	$ 24.66	$ 23.60
$ 4000.00	$ 50.13	$ 39.98	$ 35.35	$ 32.89	$ 31.47
$ 5000.00	$ 62.66	$ 49.97	$ 44.19	$ 41.11	$ 39.34
$ 10000.00	$ 125.33	$ 99.94	$ 88.37	$ 82.21	$ 78.67
$ 15000.00	$ 187.99	$ 149.92	$ 132.56	$ 123.32	$ 118.01
$ 20000.00	$ 250.65	$ 199.89	$ 176.74	$ 164.43	$ 157.34
$ 25000.00	$ 313.32	$ 249.86	$ 220.93	$ 205.54	$ 196.68
$ 30000.00	$ 375.98	$ 299.83	$ 265.11	$ 246.64	$ 236.01
$ 35000.00	$ 438.64	$ 349.81	$ 309.30	$ 287.75	$ 275.35
$ 40000.00	$ 501.31	$ 399.78	$ 353.48	$ 328.86	$ 314.68
$ 45000.00	$ 563.97	$ 449.75	$ 397.67	$ 369.96	$ 354.02
$ 50000.00	$ 626.63	$ 499.72	$ 441.86	$ 411.07	$ 393.35
$ 55000.00	$ 689.30	$ 549.70	$ 486.04	$ 452.18	$ 432.69
$ 60000.00	$ 751.96	$ 599.67	$ 530.23	$ 493.29	$ 472.02
$ 65000.00	$ 814.62	$ 649.64	$ 574.41	$ 534.39	$ 511.36
$ 70000.00	$ 877.29	$ 699.61	$ 618.60	$ 575.50	$ 550.69
$ 75000.00	$ 939.95	$ 749.59	$ 662.78	$ 616.61	$ 590.03
$ 80000.00	$1002.61	$ 799.56	$ 706.97	$ 657.71	$ 629.36
$ 85000.00	$1065.28	$ 849.53	$ 751.15	$ 698.82	$ 668.70
$ 90000.00	$1127.94	$ 899.50	$ 795.34	$ 739.93	$ 708.03
$ 95000.00	$1190.60	$ 949.48	$ 839.53	$ 781.04	$ 747.37
$100000.00	$1253.27	$ 999.45	$ 883.71	$ 822.14	$ 786.70
$125000.00	$1566.58	$1249.31	$1104.64	$1027.68	$ 983.38
$150000.00	$1879.90	$1499.17	$1325.57	$1233.22	$1180.05

YEARLY INTEREST RATE = 9.00%

PRINCIPAL	10	LOAN LIFE IN YEARS 15 20 MONTHLY PAYMENTS		25	30
$ 25.00	$ .32	$ .25	$ .22	$ .21	$ .20
$ 50.00	$ .63	$ .51	$ .45	$ .42	$ .40
$ 100.00	$ 1.27	$ 1.01	$ .90	$ .84	$ .80
$ 200.00	$ 2.53	$ 2.03	$ 1.80	$ 1.68	$ 1.61
$ 300.00	$ 3.80	$ 3.04	$ 2.70	$ 2.52	$ 2.41
$ 400.00	$ 5.07	$ 4.06	$ 3.60	$ 3.36	$ 3.22
$ 500.00	$ 6.33	$ 5.07	$ 4.50	$ 4.20	$ 4.02
$ 1000.00	$ 12.67	$ 10.14	$ 9.00	$ 8.39	$ 8.05
$ 2000.00	$ 25.34	$ 20.29	$ 17.99	$ 16.78	$ 16.09
$ 3000.00	$ 38.00	$ 30.43	$ 26.99	$ 25.18	$ 24.14
$ 4000.00	$ 50.67	$ 40.57	$ 35.99	$ 33.57	$ 32.18
$ 5000.00	$ 63.34	$ 50.71	$ 44.99	$ 41.96	$ 40.23
$ 10000.00	$ 126.68	$ 101.43	$ 89.97	$ 83.92	$ 80.46
$ 15000.00	$ 190.01	$ 152.14	$ 134.96	$ 125.88	$ 120.69
$ 20000.00	$ 253.35	$ 202.85	$ 179.95	$ 167.84	$ 160.92
$ 25000.00	$ 316.69	$ 253.57	$ 224.93	$ 209.80	$ 201.16
$ 30000.00	$ 380.03	$ 304.28	$ 269.92	$ 251.76	$ 241.39
$ 35000.00	$ 443.37	$ 354.99	$ 314.90	$ 293.72	$ 281.62
$ 40000.00	$ 506.70	$ 405.71	$ 359.89	$ 335.68	$ 321.85
$ 45000.00	$ 570.04	$ 456.42	$ 404.88	$ 377.64	$ 362.08
$ 50000.00	$ 633.38	$ 507.13	$ 449.86	$ 419.60	$ 402.31
$ 55000.00	$ 696.72	$ 557.85	$ 494.85	$ 461.56	$ 442.54
$ 60000.00	$ 760.05	$ 608.56	$ 539.84	$ 503.52	$ 482.77
$ 65000.00	$ 823.39	$ 659.27	$ 584.82	$ 545.48	$ 523.00
$ 70000.00	$ 886.73	$ 709.99	$ 629.81	$ 587.44	$ 563.24
$ 75000.00	$ 950.07	$ 760.70	$ 674.79	$ 629.40	$ 603.47
$ 80000.00	$1013.41	$ 811.41	$ 719.78	$ 671.36	$ 643.70
$ 85000.00	$1076.74	$ 862.13	$ 764.77	$ 713.32	$ 683.93
$ 90000.00	$1140.08	$ 912.84	$ 809.75	$ 755.28	$ 724.16
$ 95000.00	$1203.42	$ 963.55	$ 854.74	$ 797.24	$ 764.39
$100000.00	$1266.76	$1014.27	$ 899.73	$ 839.20	$ 804.62
$125000.00	$1583.45	$1267.83	$1124.66	$1049.00	$1005.78
$150000.00	$1900.14	$1521.40	$1349.59	$1258.79	$1206.93

YEARLY INTEREST RATE = 9.25%

PRINCIPAL	10	LOAN LIFE IN YEARS 15 20 MONTHLY PAYMENTS		25	30
$ 25.00	$ .32	$ .26	$ .23	$ .21	$ .21
$ 50.00	$ .64	$ .51	$ .46	$ .43	$ .41
$ 100.00	$ 1.28	$ 1.03	$ .92	$ .86	$ .82
$ 200.00	$ 2.56	$ 2.06	$ 1.83	$ 1.71	$ 1.65
$ 300.00	$ 3.84	$ 3.09	$ 2.75	$ 2.57	$ 2.47
$ 400.00	$ 5.12	$ 4.12	$ 3.66	$ 3.43	$ 3.29
$ 500.00	$ 6.40	$ 5.15	$ 4.58	$ 4.28	$ 4.11
$ 1000.00	$ 12.80	$ 10.29	$ 9.16	$ 8.56	$ 8.23
$ 2000.00	$ 25.61	$ 20.58	$ 18.32	$ 17.13	$ 16.45
$ 3000.00	$ 38.41	$ 30.88	$ 27.48	$ 25.69	$ 24.68
$ 4000.00	$ 51.21	$ 41.17	$ 36.63	$ 34.26	$ 32.91
$ 5000.00	$ 64.02	$ 51.46	$ 45.79	$ 42.82	$ 41.13
$ 10000.00	$ 128.03	$ 102.92	$ 91.59	$ 85.64	$ 82.27
$ 15000.00	$ 192.05	$ 154.38	$ 137.38	$ 128.46	$ 123.40
$ 20000.00	$ 256.07	$ 205.84	$ 183.17	$ 171.28	$ 164.54
$ 25000.00	$ 320.08	$ 257.30	$ 228.97	$ 214.10	$ 205.67
$ 30000.00	$ 384.10	$ 308.76	$ 274.76	$ 256.91	$ 246.80
$ 35000.00	$ 448.11	$ 360.22	$ 320.55	$ 299.73	$ 287.94
$ 40000.00	$ 512.13	$ 411.68	$ 366.35	$ 342.55	$ 329.07
$ 45000.00	$ 576.15	$ 463.14	$ 412.14	$ 385.37	$ 370.20
$ 50000.00	$ 640.16	$ 514.60	$ 457.93	$ 428.19	$ 411.34
$ 55000.00	$ 704.18	$ 566.06	$ 503.73	$ 471.01	$ 452.47
$ 60000.00	$ 768.20	$ 617.52	$ 549.52	$ 513.83	$ 493.61
$ 65000.00	$ 832.21	$ 668.97	$ 595.31	$ 556.65	$ 534.74
$ 70000.00	$ 896.23	$ 720.43	$ 641.11	$ 599.47	$ 575.87
$ 75000.00	$ 960.25	$ 771.89	$ 686.90	$ 642.29	$ 617.01
$ 80000.00	$1024.26	$ 823.35	$ 732.69	$ 685.11	$ 658.14
$ 85000.00	$1088.28	$ 874.81	$ 778.49	$ 727.92	$ 699.27
$ 90000.00	$1152.29	$ 926.27	$ 824.28	$ 770.74	$ 740.41
$ 95000.00	$1216.31	$ 977.73	$ 870.07	$ 813.56	$ 781.54
$100000.00	$1280.33	$1029.19	$ 915.87	$ 856.38	$ 822.68
$125000.00	$1600.41	$1286.49	$1144.83	$1070.48	$1028.34
$150000.00	$1920.49	$1543.79	$1373.80	$1284.57	$1234.01

YEARLY INTEREST RATE = 9.50%

LOAN LIFE IN YEARS — MONTHLY PAYMENTS

PRINCIPAL	10	15	20	25	30
$ 25.00	$ .32	$ .26	$ .23	$ .22	$ .21
$ 50.00	$ .65	$ .52	$ .47	$ .44	$ .42
$ 100.00	$ 1.29	$ 1.04	$ .93	$ .87	$ .84
$ 200.00	$ 2.59	$ 2.09	$ 1.86	$ 1.75	$ 1.68
$ 300.00	$ 3.88	$ 3.13	$ 2.80	$ 2.62	$ 2.52
$ 400.00	$ 5.18	$ 4.18	$ 3.73	$ 3.49	$ 3.36
$ 500.00	$ 6.47	$ 5.22	$ 4.66	$ 4.37	$ 4.20
$ 1000.00	$ 12.94	$ 10.44	$ 9.32	$ 8.74	$ 8.41
$ 2000.00	$ 25.88	$ 20.88	$ 18.64	$ 17.47	$ 16.82
$ 3000.00	$ 38.82	$ 31.33	$ 27.96	$ 26.21	$ 25.23
$ 4000.00	$ 51.76	$ 41.77	$ 37.29	$ 34.95	$ 33.63
$ 5000.00	$ 64.70	$ 52.21	$ 46.61	$ 43.68	$ 42.04
$ 10000.00	$ 129.40	$ 104.42	$ 93.21	$ 87.37	$ 84.09
$ 15000.00	$ 194.10	$ 156.63	$ 139.82	$ 131.05	$ 126.13
$ 20000.00	$ 258.80	$ 208.84	$ 186.43	$ 174.74	$ 168.17
$ 25000.00	$ 323.49	$ 261.06	$ 233.03	$ 218.42	$ 210.21
$ 30000.00	$ 388.19	$ 313.27	$ 279.64	$ 262.11	$ 252.26
$ 35000.00	$ 452.89	$ 365.48	$ 326.25	$ 305.79	$ 294.30
$ 40000.00	$ 517.59	$ 417.69	$ 372.85	$ 349.48	$ 336.34
$ 45000.00	$ 582.29	$ 469.90	$ 419.46	$ 393.16	$ 378.38
$ 50000.00	$ 646.99	$ 522.11	$ 466.07	$ 436.85	$ 420.43
$ 55000.00	$ 711.69	$ 574.32	$ 512.67	$ 480.53	$ 462.47
$ 60000.00	$ 776.39	$ 626.53	$ 559.28	$ 524.22	$ 504.51
$ 65000.00	$ 841.08	$ 678.75	$ 605.89	$ 567.90	$ 546.56
$ 70000.00	$ 905.78	$ 730.96	$ 652.49	$ 611.59	$ 588.60
$ 75000.00	$ 970.48	$ 783.17	$ 699.10	$ 655.27	$ 630.64
$ 80000.00	$1035.18	$ 835.38	$ 745.70	$ 698.96	$ 672.68
$ 85000.00	$1099.88	$ 887.59	$ 792.31	$ 742.64	$ 714.73
$ 90000.00	$1164.58	$ 939.80	$ 838.92	$ 786.33	$ 756.77
$ 95000.00	$1229.28	$ 992.01	$ 885.52	$ 830.01	$ 798.81
$100000.00	$1293.98	$1044.22	$ 932.13	$ 873.70	$ 840.85
$125000.00	$1617.47	$1305.28	$1165.16	$1092.12	$1051.07
$150000.00	$1940.96	$1566.34	$1398.20	$1310.54	$1261.28

YEARLY INTEREST RATE = 9.75%

LOAN LIFE IN YEARS — MONTHLY PAYMENTS

PRINCIPAL	10	15	20	25	30
$ 25.00	$ .33	$ .26	$ .24	$ .22	$ .21
$ 50.00	$ .65	$ .53	$ .47	$ .45	$ .43
$ 100.00	$ 1.31	$ 1.06	$ .95	$ .89	$ .86
$ 200.00	$ 2.62	$ 2.12	$ 1.90	$ 1.78	$ 1.72
$ 300.00	$ 3.92	$ 3.18	$ 2.85	$ 2.67	$ 2.58
$ 400.00	$ 5.23	$ 4.24	$ 3.79	$ 3.56	$ 3.44
$ 500.00	$ 6.54	$ 5.30	$ 4.74	$ 4.46	$ 4.30
$ 1000.00	$ 13.08	$ 10.59	$ 9.49	$ 8.91	$ 8.59
$ 2000.00	$ 26.15	$ 21.19	$ 18.97	$ 17.82	$ 17.18
$ 3000.00	$ 39.23	$ 31.78	$ 28.46	$ 26.73	$ 25.77
$ 4000.00	$ 52.31	$ 42.37	$ 37.94	$ 35.65	$ 34.37
$ 5000.00	$ 65.39	$ 52.97	$ 47.43	$ 44.56	$ 42.96
$ 10000.00	$ 130.77	$ 105.94	$ 94.85	$ 89.11	$ 85.92
$ 15000.00	$ 196.16	$ 158.90	$ 142.28	$ 133.67	$ 128.87
$ 20000.00	$ 261.54	$ 211.87	$ 189.70	$ 178.23	$ 171.83
$ 25000.00	$ 326.93	$ 264.84	$ 237.13	$ 222.78	$ 214.79
$ 30000.00	$ 392.31	$ 317.81	$ 284.55	$ 267.34	$ 257.75
$ 35000.00	$ 457.70	$ 370.78	$ 331.98	$ 311.90	$ 300.70
$ 40000.00	$ 523.08	$ 423.74	$ 379.41	$ 356.45	$ 343.66
$ 45000.00	$ 588.47	$ 476.71	$ 426.83	$ 401.01	$ 386.62
$ 50000.00	$ 653.85	$ 529.68	$ 474.26	$ 445.57	$ 429.58
$ 55000.00	$ 719.24	$ 582.65	$ 521.68	$ 490.13	$ 472.53
$ 60000.00	$ 784.62	$ 635.62	$ 569.11	$ 534.68	$ 515.49
$ 65000.00	$ 850.01	$ 688.59	$ 616.54	$ 579.24	$ 558.45
$ 70000.00	$ 915.39	$ 741.55	$ 663.96	$ 623.80	$ 601.41
$ 75000.00	$ 980.78	$ 794.52	$ 711.39	$ 668.35	$ 644.37
$ 80000.00	$1046.16	$ 847.49	$ 758.81	$ 712.91	$ 687.32
$ 85000.00	$1111.55	$ 900.46	$ 806.24	$ 757.47	$ 730.28
$ 90000.00	$1176.93	$ 953.43	$ 853.66	$ 802.02	$ 773.24
$ 95000.00	$1242.32	$1006.39	$ 901.09	$ 846.58	$ 816.20
$100000.00	$1307.70	$1059.36	$ 948.52	$ 891.14	$ 859.15
$125000.00	$1634.63	$1324.20	$1185.65	$1113.92	$1073.94
$150000.00	$1961.55	$1589.04	$1422.77	$1336.71	$1288.73

YEARLY INTEREST RATE = 10.00%

| | LOAN LIFE IN YEARS | | | | |
| | 10 | 15 | 20 | 25 | 30 |
PRINCIPAL			MONTHLY PAYMENTS		
$ 25.00	$ .33	$ .27	$ .24	$ .23	$ .22
$ 50.00	$ .66	$ .54	$ .48	$ .45	$ .44
$ 100.00	$ 1.32	$ 1.07	$ .97	$ .91	$ .88
$ 200.00	$ 2.64	$ 2.15	$ 1.93	$ 1.82	$ 1.76
$ 300.00	$ 3.96	$ 3.22	$ 2.90	$ 2.73	$ 2.63
$ 400.00	$ 5.29	$ 4.30	$ 3.86	$ 3.63	$ 3.51
$ 500.00	$ 6.61	$ 5.37	$ 4.83	$ 4.54	$ 4.39
$ 1000.00	$ 13.22	$ 10.75	$ 9.65	$ 9.09	$ 8.78
$ 2000.00	$ 26.43	$ 21.49	$ 19.30	$ 18.17	$ 17.55
$ 3000.00	$ 39.65	$ 32.24	$ 28.95	$ 27.26	$ 26.33
$ 4000.00	$ 52.86	$ 42.98	$ 38.60	$ 36.35	$ 35.10
$ 5000.00	$ 66.08	$ 53.73	$ 48.25	$ 45.44	$ 43.88
$ 10000.00	$ 132.15	$ 107.46	$ 96.50	$ 90.87	$ 87.76
$ 15000.00	$ 198.23	$ 161.19	$ 144.75	$ 136.31	$ 131.64
$ 20000.00	$ 264.30	$ 214.92	$ 193.00	$ 181.74	$ 175.51
$ 25000.00	$ 330.38	$ 268.65	$ 241.26	$ 227.18	$ 219.39
$ 30000.00	$ 396.45	$ 322.38	$ 289.51	$ 272.61	$ 263.27
$ 35000.00	$ 462.53	$ 376.11	$ 337.76	$ 318.05	$ 307.15
$ 40000.00	$ 528.60	$ 429.84	$ 386.01	$ 363.48	$ 351.03
$ 45000.00	$ 594.68	$ 483.57	$ 434.26	$ 408.92	$ 394.91
$ 50000.00	$ 660.75	$ 537.30	$ 482.51	$ 454.35	$ 438.79
$ 55000.00	$ 726.83	$ 591.03	$ 530.76	$ 499.79	$ 482.66
$ 60000.00	$ 792.90	$ 644.76	$ 579.01	$ 545.22	$ 526.54
$ 65000.00	$ 858.98	$ 698.49	$ 627.26	$ 590.66	$ 570.42
$ 70000.00	$ 925.06	$ 752.22	$ 675.51	$ 636.09	$ 614.30
$ 75000.00	$ 991.13	$ 805.95	$ 723.77	$ 681.53	$ 658.18
$ 80000.00	$1057.21	$ 859.68	$ 772.02	$ 726.96	$ 702.06
$ 85000.00	$1123.28	$ 913.41	$ 820.27	$ 772.40	$ 745.94
$ 90000.00	$1189.36	$ 967.14	$ 868.52	$ 817.83	$ 789.81
$ 95000.00	$1255.43	$1020.87	$ 916.77	$ 863.27	$ 833.69
$100000.00	$1321.51	$1074.60	$ 965.02	$ 908.70	$ 877.57
$125000.00	$1651.88	$1343.26	$1206.28	$1135.88	$1096.96
$150000.00	$1982.26	$1611.91	$1447.53	$1363.05	$1316.36

YEARLY INTEREST RATE = 10.25%

| | LOAN LIFE IN YEARS | | | | |
| | 10 | 15 | 20 | 25 | 30 |
PRINCIPAL			MONTHLY PAYMENTS		
$ 25.00	$ .33	$ .27	$ .25	$ .23	$ .22
$ 50.00	$ .67	$ .54	$ .49	$ .46	$ .45
$ 100.00	$ 1.34	$ 1.09	$ .98	$ .93	$ .90
$ 200.00	$ 2.67	$ 2.18	$ 1.96	$ 1.85	$ 1.79
$ 300.00	$ 4.01	$ 3.27	$ 2.94	$ 2.78	$ 2.69
$ 400.00	$ 5.34	$ 4.36	$ 3.93	$ 3.71	$ 3.58
$ 500.00	$ 6.68	$ 5.45	$ 4.91	$ 4.63	$ 4.48
$ 1000.00	$ 13.35	$ 10.90	$ 9.82	$ 9.26	$ 8.96
$ 2000.00	$ 26.71	$ 21.80	$ 19.63	$ 18.53	$ 17.92
$ 3000.00	$ 40.06	$ 32.70	$ 29.45	$ 27.79	$ 26.88
$ 4000.00	$ 53.42	$ 43.60	$ 39.27	$ 37.06	$ 35.84
$ 5000.00	$ 66.77	$ 54.50	$ 49.08	$ 46.32	$ 44.81
$ 10000.00	$ 133.54	$ 109.00	$ 98.16	$ 92.64	$ 89.61
$ 15000.00	$ 200.31	$ 163.49	$ 147.25	$ 138.96	$ 134.42
$ 20000.00	$ 267.08	$ 217.99	$ 196.33	$ 185.28	$ 179.22
$ 25000.00	$ 333.85	$ 272.49	$ 245.41	$ 231.60	$ 224.03
$ 30000.00	$ 400.62	$ 326.99	$ 294.49	$ 277.91	$ 268.83
$ 35000.00	$ 467.39	$ 381.48	$ 343.58	$ 324.23	$ 313.64
$ 40000.00	$ 534.16	$ 435.98	$ 392.66	$ 370.55	$ 358.44
$ 45000.00	$ 600.93	$ 490.48	$ 441.74	$ 416.87	$ 403.25
$ 50000.00	$ 667.69	$ 544.98	$ 490.82	$ 463.19	$ 448.05
$ 55000.00	$ 734.46	$ 599.47	$ 539.90	$ 509.51	$ 492.86
$ 60000.00	$ 801.23	$ 653.97	$ 588.99	$ 555.83	$ 537.66
$ 65000.00	$ 868.00	$ 708.47	$ 638.07	$ 602.15	$ 582.47
$ 70000.00	$ 934.77	$ 762.97	$ 687.15	$ 648.47	$ 627.27
$ 75000.00	$1001.54	$ 817.46	$ 736.23	$ 694.79	$ 672.08
$ 80000.00	$1068.31	$ 871.96	$ 785.31	$ 741.11	$ 716.88
$ 85000.00	$1135.08	$ 926.46	$ 834.40	$ 787.43	$ 761.69
$ 90000.00	$1201.85	$ 980.96	$ 883.48	$ 833.74	$ 806.49
$ 95000.00	$1268.62	$1035.45	$ 932.56	$ 880.06	$ 851.30
$100000.00	$1335.39	$1089.95	$ 981.64	$ 926.38	$ 896.10
$125000.00	$1669.24	$1362.44	$1227.05	$1157.98	$1120.13
$150000.00	$2003.08	$1634.93	$1472.46	$1389.57	$1344.15

YEARLY INTEREST RATE = 10.50%

LOAN LIFE IN YEARS

PRINCIPAL	10	15	20	25	30
			MONTHLY PAYMENTS		
$ 25.00	$ .34	$ .28	$ .25	$ .24	$ .23
$ 50.00	$ .67	$ .55	$ .50	$ .47	$ .46
$ 100.00	$ 1.35	$ 1.11	$ 1.00	$ .94	$ .91
$ 200.00	$ 2.70	$ 2.21	$ 2.00	$ 1.89	$ 1.83
$ 300.00	$ 4.05	$ 3.32	$ 3.00	$ 2.83	$ 2.74
$ 400.00	$ 5.40	$ 4.42	$ 3.99	$ 3.78	$ 3.66
$ 500.00	$ 6.75	$ 5.53	$ 4.99	$ 4.72	$ 4.57
$ 1000.00	$ 13.49	$ 11.05	$ 9.98	$ 9.44	$ 9.15
$ 2000.00	$ 26.99	$ 22.11	$ 19.97	$ 18.88	$ 18.29
$ 3000.00	$ 40.48	$ 33.16	$ 29.95	$ 28.33	$ 27.44
$ 4000.00	$ 53.97	$ 44.22	$ 39.94	$ 37.77	$ 36.59
$ 5000.00	$ 67.47	$ 55.27	$ 49.92	$ 47.21	$ 45.74
$ 10000.00	$ 134.93	$ 110.54	$ 99.84	$ 94.42	$ 91.47
$ 15000.00	$ 202.40	$ 165.81	$ 149.76	$ 141.63	$ 137.21
$ 20000.00	$ 269.87	$ 221.08	$ 199.68	$ 188.84	$ 182.95
$ 25000.00	$ 337.34	$ 276.35	$ 249.59	$ 236.05	$ 228.68
$ 30000.00	$ 404.80	$ 331.62	$ 299.51	$ 283.25	$ 274.42
$ 35000.00	$ 472.27	$ 386.89	$ 349.43	$ 330.46	$ 320.16
$ 40000.00	$ 539.74	$ 442.16	$ 399.35	$ 377.67	$ 365.90
$ 45000.00	$ 607.21	$ 497.43	$ 449.27	$ 424.88	$ 411.63
$ 50000.00	$ 674.67	$ 552.70	$ 499.19	$ 472.09	$ 457.37
$ 55000.00	$ 742.14	$ 607.97	$ 549.11	$ 519.30	$ 503.11
$ 60000.00	$ 809.61	$ 663.24	$ 599.03	$ 566.51	$ 548.84
$ 65000.00	$ 877.08	$ 718.51	$ 648.95	$ 613.72	$ 594.58
$ 70000.00	$ 944.54	$ 773.78	$ 698.87	$ 660.93	$ 640.32
$ 75000.00	$ 1012.01	$ 829.05	$ 748.78	$ 708.14	$ 686.05
$ 80000.00	$ 1079.48	$ 884.32	$ 798.70	$ 755.35	$ 731.79
$ 85000.00	$ 1146.95	$ 939.59	$ 848.62	$ 802.55	$ 777.53
$ 90000.00	$ 1214.41	$ 994.86	$ 898.54	$ 849.76	$ 823.27
$ 95000.00	$ 1281.88	$ 1050.13	$ 948.46	$ 896.97	$ 869.00
$ 100000.00	$ 1349.35	$ 1105.40	$ 998.38	$ 944.18	$ 914.74
$ 125000.00	$ 1686.69	$ 1381.75	$ 1247.97	$ 1180.23	$ 1143.42
$ 150000.00	$ 2024.02	$ 1658.10	$ 1497.57	$ 1416.27	$ 1372.11

YEARLY INTEREST RATE = 10.75%

LOAN LIFE IN YEARS

PRINCIPAL	10	15	20	25	30
			MONTHLY PAYMENTS		
$ 25.00	$ .34	$ .28	$ .25	$ .24	$ .23
$ 50.00	$ .68	$ .56	$ .51	$ .48	$ .47
$ 100.00	$ 1.36	$ 1.12	$ 1.02	$ .96	$ .93
$ 200.00	$ 2.73	$ 2.24	$ 2.03	$ 1.92	$ 1.87
$ 300.00	$ 4.09	$ 3.36	$ 3.05	$ 2.89	$ 2.80
$ 400.00	$ 5.45	$ 4.48	$ 4.06	$ 3.85	$ 3.73
$ 500.00	$ 6.82	$ 5.60	$ 5.08	$ 4.81	$ 4.67
$ 1000.00	$ 13.63	$ 11.21	$ 10.15	$ 9.62	$ 9.33
$ 2000.00	$ 27.27	$ 22.42	$ 20.30	$ 19.24	$ 18.67
$ 3000.00	$ 40.90	$ 33.63	$ 30.46	$ 28.86	$ 28.00
$ 4000.00	$ 54.54	$ 44.84	$ 40.61	$ 38.48	$ 37.34
$ 5000.00	$ 68.17	$ 56.05	$ 50.76	$ 48.10	$ 46.67
$ 10000.00	$ 136.34	$ 112.09	$ 101.52	$ 96.21	$ 93.35
$ 15000.00	$ 204.51	$ 168.14	$ 152.28	$ 144.31	$ 140.02
$ 20000.00	$ 272.68	$ 224.19	$ 203.05	$ 192.42	$ 186.70
$ 25000.00	$ 340.85	$ 280.24	$ 253.81	$ 240.52	$ 233.37
$ 30000.00	$ 409.02	$ 336.28	$ 304.57	$ 288.63	$ 280.04
$ 35000.00	$ 477.19	$ 392.33	$ 355.33	$ 336.73	$ 326.72
$ 40000.00	$ 545.35	$ 448.38	$ 406.09	$ 384.84	$ 373.39
$ 45000.00	$ 613.52	$ 504.43	$ 456.85	$ 432.94	$ 420.07
$ 50000.00	$ 681.69	$ 560.47	$ 507.61	$ 481.05	$ 466.74
$ 55000.00	$ 749.86	$ 616.52	$ 558.38	$ 529.15	$ 513.41
$ 60000.00	$ 818.03	$ 672.57	$ 609.14	$ 577.26	$ 560.09
$ 65000.00	$ 886.20	$ 728.62	$ 659.90	$ 625.36	$ 606.76
$ 70000.00	$ 954.37	$ 784.66	$ 710.66	$ 673.46	$ 653.44
$ 75000.00	$ 1022.54	$ 840.71	$ 761.42	$ 721.57	$ 700.11
$ 80000.00	$ 1090.71	$ 896.76	$ 812.18	$ 769.67	$ 746.78
$ 85000.00	$ 1158.88	$ 952.81	$ 862.94	$ 817.78	$ 793.46
$ 90000.00	$ 1227.05	$ 1008.85	$ 913.71	$ 865.88	$ 840.13
$ 95000.00	$ 1295.22	$ 1064.90	$ 964.47	$ 913.99	$ 886.81
$ 100000.00	$ 1363.39	$ 1120.95	$ 1015.23	$ 962.09	$ 933.48
$ 125000.00	$ 1704.23	$ 1401.18	$ 1269.04	$ 1202.62	$ 1166.85
$ 150000.00	$ 2045.08	$ 1681.42	$ 1522.84	$ 1443.14	$ 1400.22

YEARLY INTEREST RATE = 11.00%

LOAN LIFE IN YEARS

PRINCIPAL	10	15	20 MONTHLY PAYMENTS	25	30
$ 25.00	$ .34	$ .28	$ .26	$ .25	$ .24
$ 50.00	$ .69	$ .57	$ .52	$ .49	$ .48
$ 100.00	$ 1.38	$ 1.14	$ 1.03	$ .98	$ .95
$ 200.00	$ 2.75	$ 2.27	$ 2.06	$ 1.96	$ 1.90
$ 300.00	$ 4.13	$ 3.41	$ 3.10	$ 2.94	$ 2.86
$ 400.00	$ 5.51	$ 4.55	$ 4.13	$ 3.92	$ 3.81
$ 500.00	$ 6.89	$ 5.68	$ 5.16	$ 4.90	$ 4.76
$ 1000.00	$ 13.77	$ 11.37	$ 10.32	$ 9.80	$ 9.52
$ 2000.00	$ 27.55	$ 22.73	$ 20.64	$ 19.60	$ 19.05
$ 3000.00	$ 41.32	$ 34.10	$ 30.97	$ 29.40	$ 28.57
$ 4000.00	$ 55.10	$ 45.46	$ 41.29	$ 39.20	$ 38.09
$ 5000.00	$ 68.87	$ 56.83	$ 51.61	$ 49.01	$ 47.62
$ 10000.00	$ 137.75	$ 113.66	$ 103.22	$ 98.01	$ 95.23
$ 15000.00	$ 206.62	$ 170.49	$ 154.83	$ 147.02	$ 142.85
$ 20000.00	$ 275.50	$ 227.32	$ 206.44	$ 196.02	$ 190.46
$ 25000.00	$ 344.37	$ 284.15	$ 258.05	$ 245.03	$ 238.08
$ 30000.00	$ 413.25	$ 340.98	$ 309.66	$ 294.03	$ 285.70
$ 35000.00	$ 482.12	$ 397.81	$ 361.27	$ 343.04	$ 333.31
$ 40000.00	$ 551.00	$ 454.64	$ 412.88	$ 392.05	$ 380.93
$ 45000.00	$ 619.87	$ 511.47	$ 464.48	$ 441.05	$ 428.55
$ 50000.00	$ 688.75	$ 568.30	$ 516.09	$ 490.06	$ 476.16
$ 55000.00	$ 757.62	$ 625.13	$ 567.70	$ 539.06	$ 523.78
$ 60000.00	$ 826.50	$ 681.96	$ 619.31	$ 588.07	$ 571.39
$ 65000.00	$ 895.37	$ 738.79	$ 670.92	$ 637.07	$ 619.01
$ 70000.00	$ 964.25	$ 795.62	$ 722.53	$ 686.08	$ 666.63
$ 75000.00	$1033.12	$ 852.45	$ 774.14	$ 735.08	$ 714.24
$ 80000.00	$1102.00	$ 909.28	$ 825.75	$ 784.09	$ 761.86
$ 85000.00	$1170.87	$ 966.11	$ 877.36	$ 833.10	$ 809.47
$ 90000.00	$1239.75	$1022.94	$ 928.97	$ 882.10	$ 857.09
$ 95000.00	$1308.62	$1079.77	$ 980.58	$ 931.11	$ 904.71
$100000.00	$1377.50	$1136.60	$1032.19	$ 980.11	$ 952.32
$125000.00	$1721.87	$1420.75	$1290.24	$1225.14	$1190.40
$150000.00	$2066.25	$1704.89	$1548.28	$1470.17	$1428.48

YEARLY INTEREST RATE = 11.25%

LOAN LIFE IN YEARS

PRINCIPAL	10	15	20 MONTHLY PAYMENTS	25	30
$ 25.00	$ .35	$ .29	$ .26	$ .25	$ .24
$ 50.00	$ .70	$ .58	$ .52	$ .50	$ .49
$ 100.00	$ 1.39	$ 1.15	$ 1.05	$ 1.00	$ .97
$ 200.00	$ 2.78	$ 2.30	$ 2.10	$ 2.00	$ 1.94
$ 300.00	$ 4.18	$ 3.46	$ 3.15	$ 2.99	$ 2.91
$ 400.00	$ 5.57	$ 4.61	$ 4.20	$ 3.99	$ 3.89
$ 500.00	$ 6.96	$ 5.76	$ 5.25	$ 4.99	$ 4.86
$ 1000.00	$ 13.92	$ 11.52	$ 10.49	$ 9.98	$ 9.71
$ 2000.00	$ 27.83	$ 23.05	$ 20.99	$ 19.96	$ 19.43
$ 3000.00	$ 41.75	$ 34.57	$ 31.48	$ 29.95	$ 29.14
$ 4000.00	$ 55.67	$ 46.09	$ 41.97	$ 39.93	$ 38.85
$ 5000.00	$ 69.58	$ 57.62	$ 52.46	$ 49.91	$ 48.56
$ 10000.00	$ 139.17	$ 115.23	$ 104.93	$ 99.82	$ 97.13
$ 15000.00	$ 208.75	$ 172.85	$ 157.39	$ 149.74	$ 145.69
$ 20000.00	$ 278.34	$ 230.47	$ 209.85	$ 199.65	$ 194.25
$ 25000.00	$ 347.92	$ 288.09	$ 262.31	$ 249.56	$ 242.82
$ 30000.00	$ 417.51	$ 345.70	$ 314.78	$ 299.47	$ 291.38
$ 35000.00	$ 487.09	$ 403.32	$ 367.24	$ 349.38	$ 339.94
$ 40000.00	$ 556.68	$ 460.94	$ 419.70	$ 399.30	$ 388.50
$ 45000.00	$ 626.26	$ 518.55	$ 472.17	$ 449.21	$ 437.07
$ 50000.00	$ 695.84	$ 576.17	$ 524.63	$ 499.12	$ 485.63
$ 55000.00	$ 765.43	$ 633.79	$ 577.09	$ 549.03	$ 534.19
$ 60000.00	$ 835.01	$ 691.41	$ 629.55	$ 598.94	$ 582.76
$ 65000.00	$ 904.60	$ 749.02	$ 682.02	$ 648.86	$ 631.32
$ 70000.00	$ 974.18	$ 806.64	$ 734.48	$ 698.77	$ 679.88
$ 75000.00	$1043.77	$ 864.26	$ 786.94	$ 748.68	$ 728.45
$ 80000.00	$1113.35	$ 921.88	$ 839.40	$ 798.59	$ 777.01
$ 85000.00	$1182.94	$ 979.49	$ 891.87	$ 848.50	$ 825.57
$ 90000.00	$1252.52	$1037.11	$ 944.33	$ 898.42	$ 874.13
$ 95000.00	$1322.10	$1094.73	$ 996.79	$ 948.33	$ 922.70
$100000.00	$1391.69	$1152.34	$1049.26	$ 998.24	$ 971.26
$125000.00	$1739.61	$1440.43	$1311.57	$1247.80	$1214.08
$150000.00	$2087.53	$1728.52	$1573.88	$1497.36	$1456.89

YEARLY INTEREST RATE = 11.50%

LOAN LIFE IN YEARS

PRINCIPAL	10	15	20	25	30
			MONTHLY PAYMENTS		
$ 25.00	$ .35	$ .29	$ .27	$ .25	$ .25
$ 50.00	$ .70	$ .58	$ .53	$ .51	$ .50
$ 100.00	$ 1.41	$ 1.17	$ 1.07	$ 1.02	$ .99
$ 200.00	$ 2.81	$ 2.34	$ 2.13	$ 2.03	$ 1.98
$ 300.00	$ 4.22	$ 3.50	$ 3.20	$ 3.05	$ 2.97
$ 400.00	$ 5.62	$ 4.67	$ 4.27	$ 4.07	$ 3.96
$ 500.00	$ 7.03	$ 5.84	$ 5.33	$ 5.08	$ 4.95
$ 1000.00	$ 14.06	$ 11.68	$ 10.66	$ 10.16	$ 9.90
$ 2000.00	$ 28.12	$ 23.36	$ 21.33	$ 20.33	$ 19.81
$ 3000.00	$ 42.18	$ 35.05	$ 31.99	$ 30.49	$ 29.71
$ 4000.00	$ 56.24	$ 46.73	$ 42.66	$ 40.66	$ 39.61
$ 5000.00	$ 70.30	$ 58.41	$ 53.32	$ 50.82	$ 49.51
$ 10000.00	$ 140.60	$ 116.82	$ 106.64	$ 101.65	$ 99.03
$ 15000.00	$ 210.89	$ 175.23	$ 159.96	$ 152.47	$ 148.54
$ 20000.00	$ 281.19	$ 233.64	$ 213.29	$ 203.29	$ 198.06
$ 25000.00	$ 351.49	$ 292.05	$ 266.61	$ 254.12	$ 247.57
$ 30000.00	$ 421.79	$ 350.46	$ 319.93	$ 304.94	$ 297.09
$ 35000.00	$ 492.08	$ 408.87	$ 373.25	$ 355.76	$ 346.60
$ 40000.00	$ 562.38	$ 467.28	$ 426.57	$ 406.59	$ 396.12
$ 45000.00	$ 632.68	$ 525.69	$ 479.89	$ 457.41	$ 445.63
$ 50000.00	$ 702.98	$ 584.09	$ 533.21	$ 508.23	$ 495.15
$ 55000.00	$ 773.27	$ 642.50	$ 586.54	$ 559.06	$ 544.66
$ 60000.00	$ 843.57	$ 700.91	$ 639.86	$ 609.88	$ 594.17
$ 65000.00	$ 913.87	$ 759.32	$ 693.18	$ 660.70	$ 643.69
$ 70000.00	$ 984.17	$ 817.73	$ 746.50	$ 711.53	$ 693.20
$ 75000.00	$1054.47	$ 876.14	$ 799.82	$ 762.35	$ 742.72
$ 80000.00	$1124.76	$ 934.55	$ 853.14	$ 813.17	$ 792.23
$ 85000.00	$1195.06	$ 992.96	$ 906.46	$ 864.00	$ 841.75
$ 90000.00	$1265.36	$1051.37	$ 959.79	$ 914.82	$ 891.26
$ 95000.00	$1335.66	$1109.78	$1013.11	$ 965.65	$ 940.78
$100000.00	$1405.95	$1168.19	$1066.43	$1016.47	$ 990.29
$125000.00	$1757.44	$1460.24	$1333.04	$1270.59	$1237.86
$150000.00	$2108.93	$1752.28	$1599.64	$1524.70	$1485.44

YEARLY INTEREST RATE = 11.75%

LOAN LIFE IN YEARS

PRINCIPAL	10	15	20	25	30
			MONTHLY PAYMENTS		
$ 25.00	$ .36	$ .30	$ .27	$ .26	$ .25
$ 50.00	$ .71	$ .59	$ .54	$ .52	$ .50
$ 100.00	$ 1.42	$ 1.18	$ 1.08	$ 1.03	$ 1.01
$ 200.00	$ 2.84	$ 2.37	$ 2.17	$ 2.07	$ 2.02
$ 300.00	$ 4.26	$ 3.55	$ 3.25	$ 3.10	$ 3.03
$ 400.00	$ 5.68	$ 4.74	$ 4.33	$ 4.14	$ 4.04
$ 500.00	$ 7.10	$ 5.92	$ 5.42	$ 5.17	$ 5.05
$ 1000.00	$ 14.20	$ 11.84	$ 10.84	$ 10.35	$ 10.09
$ 2000.00	$ 28.41	$ 23.68	$ 21.67	$ 20.70	$ 20.19
$ 3000.00	$ 42.61	$ 35.52	$ 32.51	$ 31.04	$ 30.28
$ 4000.00	$ 56.81	$ 47.37	$ 43.35	$ 41.39	$ 40.38
$ 5000.00	$ 71.01	$ 59.21	$ 54.19	$ 51.74	$ 50.47
$ 10000.00	$ 142.03	$ 118.41	$ 108.37	$ 103.48	$ 100.94
$ 15000.00	$ 213.04	$ 177.62	$ 162.56	$ 155.22	$ 151.41
$ 20000.00	$ 284.06	$ 236.83	$ 216.74	$ 206.96	$ 201.88
$ 25000.00	$ 355.07	$ 296.03	$ 270.93	$ 258.70	$ 252.35
$ 30000.00	$ 426.09	$ 355.24	$ 325.11	$ 310.44	$ 302.82
$ 35000.00	$ 497.10	$ 414.45	$ 379.30	$ 362.18	$ 353.29
$ 40000.00	$ 568.12	$ 473.65	$ 433.48	$ 413.92	$ 403.76
$ 45000.00	$ 639.13	$ 532.86	$ 487.67	$ 465.66	$ 454.23
$ 50000.00	$ 710.15	$ 592.07	$ 541.85	$ 517.40	$ 504.70
$ 55000.00	$ 781.16	$ 651.27	$ 596.04	$ 569.14	$ 555.18
$ 60000.00	$ 852.18	$ 710.48	$ 650.22	$ 620.88	$ 605.65
$ 65000.00	$ 923.19	$ 769.69	$ 704.41	$ 672.62	$ 656.12
$ 70000.00	$ 994.21	$ 828.89	$ 758.59	$ 724.36	$ 706.59
$ 75000.00	$1065.22	$ 888.10	$ 812.78	$ 776.10	$ 757.06
$ 80000.00	$1136.24	$ 947.30	$ 866.97	$ 827.84	$ 807.53
$ 85000.00	$1207.25	$1006.51	$ 921.15	$ 879.58	$ 858.00
$ 90000.00	$1278.26	$1065.72	$ 975.34	$ 931.32	$ 908.47
$ 95000.00	$1349.28	$1124.92	$1029.52	$ 983.06	$ 958.94
$100000.00	$1420.29	$1184.13	$1083.71	$1034.80	$1009.41
$125000.00	$1775.37	$1480.16	$1354.63	$1293.50	$1261.76
$150000.00	$2130.44	$1776.20	$1625.56	$1552.20	$1514.11

YEARLY INTEREST RATE = 12.00%

LOAN LIFE IN YEARS

PRINCIPAL	10	15	20	25	30
			MONTHLY PAYMENTS		
$ 25.00	$ .36	$ .30	$ .28	$ .26	$ .26
$ 50.00	$ .72	$ .60	$ .55	$ .53	$ .51
$ 100.00	$ 1.43	$ 1.20	$ 1.10	$ 1.05	$ 1.03
$ 200.00	$ 2.87	$ 2.40	$ 2.20	$ 2.11	$ 2.06
$ 300.00	$ 4.30	$ 3.60	$ 3.30	$ 3.16	$ 3.09
$ 400.00	$ 5.74	$ 4.80	$ 4.40	$ 4.21	$ 4.11
$ 500.00	$ 7.17	$ 6.00	$ 5.51	$ 5.27	$ 5.14
$ 1000.00	$ 14.35	$ 12.00	$ 11.01	$ 10.53	$ 10.29
$ 2000.00	$ 28.69	$ 24.00	$ 22.02	$ 21.06	$ 20.57
$ 3000.00	$ 43.04	$ 36.01	$ 33.03	$ 31.60	$ 30.86
$ 4000.00	$ 57.39	$ 48.01	$ 44.04	$ 42.13	$ 41.14
$ 5000.00	$ 71.74	$ 60.01	$ 55.05	$ 52.66	$ 51.43
$ 10000.00	$ 143.47	$ 120.02	$ 110.11	$ 105.32	$ 102.86
$ 15000.00	$ 215.21	$ 180.03	$ 165.16	$ 157.98	$ 154.29
$ 20000.00	$ 286.94	$ 240.03	$ 220.22	$ 210.64	$ 205.72
$ 25000.00	$ 358.68	$ 300.04	$ 275.27	$ 263.31	$ 257.15
$ 30000.00	$ 430.41	$ 360.05	$ 330.33	$ 315.97	$ 308.58
$ 35000.00	$ 502.15	$ 420.06	$ 385.38	$ 368.63	$ 360.01
$ 40000.00	$ 573.88	$ 480.07	$ 440.43	$ 421.29	$ 411.44
$ 45000.00	$ 645.62	$ 540.08	$ 495.49	$ 473.95	$ 462.88
$ 50000.00	$ 717.35	$ 600.08	$ 550.54	$ 526.61	$ 514.31
$ 55000.00	$ 789.09	$ 660.09	$ 605.60	$ 579.27	$ 565.74
$ 60000.00	$ 860.83	$ 720.10	$ 660.65	$ 631.93	$ 617.17
$ 65000.00	$ 932.56	$ 780.11	$ 715.71	$ 684.60	$ 668.60
$ 70000.00	$ 1004.30	$ 840.12	$ 770.76	$ 737.26	$ 720.03
$ 75000.00	$ 1076.03	$ 900.13	$ 825.81	$ 789.92	$ 771.46
$ 80000.00	$ 1147.77	$ 960.13	$ 880.87	$ 842.58	$ 822.89
$ 85000.00	$ 1219.50	$ 1020.14	$ 935.92	$ 895.24	$ 874.32
$ 90000.00	$ 1291.24	$ 1080.15	$ 990.98	$ 947.90	$ 925.75
$ 95000.00	$ 1362.97	$ 1140.16	$ 1046.03	$ 1000.56	$ 977.18
$ 100000.00	$ 1434.71	$ 1200.17	$ 1101.09	$ 1053.22	$ 1028.61
$ 125000.00	$ 1793.39	$ 1500.21	$ 1376.36	$ 1316.53	$ 1285.77
$ 150000.00	$ 2152.06	$ 1800.25	$ 1651.63	$ 1579.84	$ 1542.92

YEARLY INTEREST RATE = 12.25%

LOAN LIFE IN YEARS

PRINCIPAL	10	15	20	25	30
			MONTHLY PAYMENTS		
$ 25.00	$ .36	$ .30	$ .28	$ .27	$ .26
$ 50.00	$ .72	$ .61	$ .56	$ .54	$ .52
$ 100.00	$ 1.45	$ 1.22	$ 1.12	$ 1.07	$ 1.05
$ 200.00	$ 2.90	$ 2.43	$ 2.24	$ 2.14	$ 2.10
$ 300.00	$ 4.35	$ 3.65	$ 3.36	$ 3.22	$ 3.14
$ 400.00	$ 5.80	$ 4.87	$ 4.47	$ 4.29	$ 4.19
$ 500.00	$ 7.25	$ 6.08	$ 5.59	$ 5.36	$ 5.24
$ 1000.00	$ 14.49	$ 12.16	$ 11.19	$ 10.72	$ 10.48
$ 2000.00	$ 28.98	$ 24.33	$ 22.37	$ 21.43	$ 20.96
$ 3000.00	$ 43.48	$ 36.49	$ 33.56	$ 32.15	$ 31.44
$ 4000.00	$ 57.97	$ 48.65	$ 44.74	$ 42.87	$ 41.92
$ 5000.00	$ 72.46	$ 60.81	$ 55.93	$ 53.59	$ 52.39
$ 10000.00	$ 144.92	$ 121.63	$ 111.86	$ 107.17	$ 104.79
$ 15000.00	$ 217.38	$ 182.44	$ 167.78	$ 160.76	$ 157.18
$ 20000.00	$ 289.84	$ 243.26	$ 223.71	$ 214.35	$ 209.58
$ 25000.00	$ 362.30	$ 304.07	$ 279.64	$ 267.94	$ 261.97
$ 30000.00	$ 434.76	$ 364.89	$ 335.57	$ 321.52	$ 314.37
$ 35000.00	$ 507.22	$ 425.70	$ 391.50	$ 375.11	$ 366.76
$ 40000.00	$ 579.68	$ 486.52	$ 447.43	$ 428.70	$ 419.16
$ 45000.00	$ 652.14	$ 547.33	$ 503.35	$ 482.28	$ 471.55
$ 50000.00	$ 724.60	$ 608.15	$ 559.28	$ 535.87	$ 523.95
$ 55000.00	$ 797.06	$ 668.96	$ 615.21	$ 589.46	$ 576.34
$ 60000.00	$ 869.52	$ 729.78	$ 671.14	$ 643.05	$ 628.74
$ 65000.00	$ 941.98	$ 790.59	$ 727.07	$ 696.63	$ 681.13
$ 70000.00	$ 1014.44	$ 851.41	$ 782.99	$ 750.22	$ 733.53
$ 75000.00	$ 1086.90	$ 912.22	$ 838.92	$ 803.81	$ 785.92
$ 80000.00	$ 1159.36	$ 973.04	$ 894.85	$ 857.39	$ 838.32
$ 85000.00	$ 1231.82	$ 1033.85	$ 950.78	$ 910.98	$ 890.71
$ 90000.00	$ 1304.28	$ 1094.67	$ 1006.71	$ 964.57	$ 943.11
$ 95000.00	$ 1376.74	$ 1155.48	$ 1062.64	$ 1018.16	$ 995.50
$ 100000.00	$ 1449.20	$ 1216.30	$ 1118.56	$ 1071.74	$ 1047.90
$ 125000.00	$ 1811.50	$ 1520.37	$ 1398.21	$ 1339.68	$ 1309.87
$ 150000.00	$ 2173.80	$ 1824.45	$ 1677.85	$ 1607.62	$ 1571.84

YEARLY INTEREST RATE = 12.50%

LOAN LIFE IN YEARS

PRINCIPAL	10	15	20	25	30
			MONTHLY PAYMENTS		
$ 25.00	$ .37	$ .31	$ .28	$ .27	$ .27
$ 50.00	$ .73	$ .62	$ .57	$ .55	$ .53
$ 100.00	$ 1.46	$ 1.23	$ 1.14	$ 1.09	$ 1.07
$ 200.00	$ 2.93	$ 2.47	$ 2.27	$ 2.18	$ 2.13
$ 300.00	$ 4.39	$ 3.70	$ 3.41	$ 3.27	$ 3.20
$ 400.00	$ 5.86	$ 4.93	$ 4.54	$ 4.36	$ 4.27
$ 500.00	$ 7.32	$ 6.16	$ 5.68	$ 5.45	$ 5.34
$ 1000.00	$ 14.64	$ 12.33	$ 11.36	$ 10.90	$ 10.67
$ 2000.00	$ 29.28	$ 24.65	$ 22.72	$ 21.81	$ 21.35
$ 3000.00	$ 43.91	$ 36.98	$ 34.08	$ 32.71	$ 32.02
$ 4000.00	$ 58.55	$ 49.30	$ 45.45	$ 43.61	$ 42.69
$ 5000.00	$ 73.19	$ 61.63	$ 56.81	$ 54.52	$ 53.36
$ 10000.00	$ 146.38	$ 123.25	$ 113.61	$ 109.04	$ 106.73
$ 15000.00	$ 219.56	$ 184.88	$ 170.42	$ 163.55	$ 160.09
$ 20000.00	$ 292.75	$ 246.50	$ 227.23	$ 218.07	$ 213.45
$ 25000.00	$ 365.94	$ 308.13	$ 284.04	$ 272.59	$ 266.81
$ 30000.00	$ 439.13	$ 369.76	$ 340.84	$ 327.11	$ 320.18
$ 35000.00	$ 512.32	$ 431.38	$ 397.65	$ 381.62	$ 373.54
$ 40000.00	$ 585.50	$ 493.01	$ 454.46	$ 436.14	$ 426.90
$ 45000.00	$ 658.69	$ 554.63	$ 511.26	$ 490.66	$ 480.27
$ 50000.00	$ 731.88	$ 616.26	$ 568.07	$ 545.18	$ 533.63
$ 55000.00	$ 805.07	$ 677.89	$ 624.88	$ 599.69	$ 586.99
$ 60000.00	$ 878.26	$ 739.51	$ 681.68	$ 654.21	$ 640.35
$ 65000.00	$ 951.44	$ 801.14	$ 738.49	$ 708.73	$ 693.72
$ 70000.00	$1024.63	$ 862.77	$ 795.30	$ 763.25	$ 747.08
$ 75000.00	$1097.82	$ 924.39	$ 852.11	$ 817.77	$ 800.44
$ 80000.00	$1171.01	$ 986.02	$ 908.91	$ 872.28	$ 853.81
$ 85000.00	$1244.20	$1047.64	$ 965.72	$ 926.80	$ 907.17
$ 90000.00	$1317.39	$1109.27	$1022.53	$ 981.32	$ 960.53
$ 95000.00	$1390.57	$1170.90	$1079.33	$1035.84	$1013.89
$100000.00	$1463.76	$1232.52	$1136.14	$1090.35	$1067.26
$125000.00	$1829.70	$1540.65	$1420.18	$1362.94	$1334.07
$150000.00	$2195.64	$1848.78	$1704.21	$1635.53	$1600.89

YEARLY INTEREST RATE = 12.75%

LOAN LIFE IN YEARS

PRINCIPAL	10	15	20	25	30
			MONTHLY PAYMENTS		
$ 25.00	$ .37	$ .31	$ .29	$ .28	$ .27
$ 50.00	$ .74	$ .62	$ .58	$ .55	$ .54
$ 100.00	$ 1.48	$ 1.25	$ 1.15	$ 1.11	$ 1.09
$ 200.00	$ 2.96	$ 2.50	$ 2.31	$ 2.22	$ 2.17
$ 300.00	$ 4.44	$ 3.75	$ 3.46	$ 3.33	$ 3.26
$ 400.00	$ 5.91	$ 5.00	$ 4.62	$ 4.44	$ 4.35
$ 500.00	$ 7.39	$ 6.24	$ 5.77	$ 5.55	$ 5.43
$ 1000.00	$ 14.78	$ 12.49	$ 11.54	$ 11.09	$ 10.87
$ 2000.00	$ 29.57	$ 24.98	$ 23.08	$ 22.18	$ 21.73
$ 3000.00	$ 44.35	$ 37.47	$ 34.61	$ 33.27	$ 32.60
$ 4000.00	$ 59.14	$ 49.95	$ 46.15	$ 44.36	$ 43.47
$ 5000.00	$ 73.92	$ 62.44	$ 57.69	$ 55.45	$ 54.33
$ 10000.00	$ 147.84	$ 124.88	$ 115.38	$ 110.91	$ 108.67
$ 15000.00	$ 221.76	$ 187.33	$ 173.07	$ 166.36	$ 163.00
$ 20000.00	$ 295.68	$ 249.77	$ 230.76	$ 221.81	$ 217.34
$ 25000.00	$ 369.60	$ 312.21	$ 288.45	$ 277.26	$ 271.67
$ 30000.00	$ 443.52	$ 374.65	$ 346.14	$ 332.72	$ 326.01
$ 35000.00	$ 517.44	$ 437.09	$ 403.83	$ 388.17	$ 380.34
$ 40000.00	$ 591.36	$ 499.53	$ 461.52	$ 443.62	$ 434.68
$ 45000.00	$ 665.28	$ 561.98	$ 519.22	$ 499.07	$ 489.01
$ 50000.00	$ 739.20	$ 624.42	$ 576.91	$ 554.53	$ 543.35
$ 55000.00	$ 813.12	$ 686.86	$ 634.60	$ 609.98	$ 597.68
$ 60000.00	$ 887.04	$ 749.30	$ 692.29	$ 665.43	$ 652.02
$ 65000.00	$ 960.96	$ 811.74	$ 749.98	$ 720.88	$ 706.35
$ 70000.00	$1034.88	$ 874.19	$ 807.67	$ 776.34	$ 760.68
$ 75000.00	$1108.80	$ 936.63	$ 865.36	$ 831.79	$ 815.02
$ 80000.00	$1182.72	$ 999.07	$ 923.05	$ 887.24	$ 869.35
$ 85000.00	$1256.64	$1061.51	$ 980.74	$ 942.69	$ 923.69
$ 90000.00	$1330.56	$1123.95	$1038.43	$ 998.15	$ 978.02
$ 95000.00	$1404.48	$1186.39	$1096.12	$1053.60	$1032.36
$100000.00	$1478.40	$1248.84	$1153.81	$1109.05	$1086.69
$125000.00	$1848.00	$1561.05	$1442.26	$1386.31	$1358.37
$150000.00	$2217.60	$1873.25	$1730.72	$1663.58	$1630.04

YEARLY INTEREST RATE = 13.00%

LOAN LIFE IN YEARS

PRINCIPAL	10	15	20	25	30
		MONTHLY PAYMENTS			
$ 25.00	$ .37	$ .32	$ .29	$ .28	$ .28
$ 50.00	$ .75	$ .63	$ .59	$ .56	$ .55
$ 100.00	$ 1.49	$ 1.27	$ 1.17	$ 1.13	$ 1.11
$ 200.00	$ 2.99	$ 2.53	$ 2.34	$ 2.26	$ 2.21
$ 300.00	$ 4.48	$ 3.80	$ 3.51	$ 3.38	$ 3.32
$ 400.00	$ 5.97	$ 5.06	$ 4.69	$ 4.51	$ 4.42
$ 500.00	$ 7.47	$ 6.33	$ 5.86	$ 5.64	$ 5.53
$ 1000.00	$ 14.93	$ 12.65	$ 11.72	$ 11.28	$ 11.06
$ 2000.00	$ 29.86	$ 25.30	$ 23.43	$ 22.56	$ 22.12
$ 3000.00	$ 44.79	$ 37.96	$ 35.15	$ 33.84	$ 33.19
$ 4000.00	$ 59.72	$ 50.61	$ 46.86	$ 45.11	$ 44.25
$ 5000.00	$ 74.66	$ 63.26	$ 58.58	$ 56.39	$ 55.31
$ 10000.00	$ 149.31	$ 126.52	$ 117.16	$ 112.78	$ 110.62
$ 15000.00	$ 223.97	$ 189.79	$ 175.74	$ 169.18	$ 165.93
$ 20000.00	$ 298.62	$ 253.05	$ 234.32	$ 225.57	$ 221.24
$ 25000.00	$ 373.28	$ 316.31	$ 292.89	$ 281.96	$ 276.55
$ 30000.00	$ 447.93	$ 379.57	$ 351.47	$ 338.35	$ 331.86
$ 35000.00	$ 522.59	$ 442.83	$ 410.05	$ 394.74	$ 387.17
$ 40000.00	$ 597.24	$ 506.10	$ 468.63	$ 451.13	$ 442.48
$ 45000.00	$ 671.90	$ 569.36	$ 527.21	$ 507.53	$ 497.79
$ 50000.00	$ 746.55	$ 632.62	$ 585.79	$ 563.92	$ 553.10
$ 55000.00	$ 821.21	$ 695.88	$ 644.37	$ 620.31	$ 608.41
$ 60000.00	$ 895.86	$ 759.15	$ 702.95	$ 676.70	$ 663.72
$ 65000.00	$ 970.52	$ 822.41	$ 761.52	$ 733.09	$ 719.03
$ 70000.00	$ 1045.17	$ 885.67	$ 820.10	$ 789.48	$ 774.34
$ 75000.00	$ 1119.83	$ 948.93	$ 878.68	$ 845.88	$ 829.65
$ 80000.00	$ 1194.49	$ 1012.19	$ 937.26	$ 902.27	$ 884.96
$ 85000.00	$ 1269.14	$ 1075.46	$ 995.84	$ 958.66	$ 940.27
$ 90000.00	$ 1343.80	$ 1138.72	$ 1054.42	$ 1015.05	$ 995.58
$ 95000.00	$ 1418.45	$ 1201.98	$ 1113.00	$ 1071.44	$ 1050.89
$ 100000.00	$ 1493.11	$ 1265.24	$ 1171.58	$ 1127.83	$ 1106.20
$ 125000.00	$ 1866.38	$ 1581.55	$ 1464.47	$ 1409.79	$ 1382.75
$ 150000.00	$ 2239.66	$ 1897.86	$ 1757.36	$ 1691.75	$ 1659.30

YEARLY INTEREST RATE = 13.25%

LOAN LIFE IN YEARS

PRINCIPAL	10	15	20	25	30
		MONTHLY PAYMENTS			
$ 25.00	$ .38	$ .32	$ .30	$ .29	$ .28
$ 50.00	$ .75	$ .64	$ .59	$ .57	$ .56
$ 100.00	$ 1.51	$ 1.28	$ 1.19	$ 1.15	$ 1.13
$ 200.00	$ 3.02	$ 2.56	$ 2.38	$ 2.29	$ 2.25
$ 300.00	$ 4.52	$ 3.85	$ 3.57	$ 3.44	$ 3.38
$ 400.00	$ 6.03	$ 5.13	$ 4.76	$ 4.59	$ 4.50
$ 500.00	$ 7.54	$ 6.41	$ 5.95	$ 5.73	$ 5.63
$ 1000.00	$ 15.08	$ 12.82	$ 11.89	$ 11.47	$ 11.26
$ 2000.00	$ 30.16	$ 25.63	$ 23.79	$ 22.93	$ 22.52
$ 3000.00	$ 45.24	$ 38.45	$ 35.68	$ 34.40	$ 33.77
$ 4000.00	$ 60.32	$ 51.27	$ 47.58	$ 45.87	$ 45.03
$ 5000.00	$ 75.39	$ 64.09	$ 59.47	$ 57.33	$ 56.29
$ 10000.00	$ 150.79	$ 128.17	$ 118.94	$ 114.67	$ 112.58
$ 15000.00	$ 226.18	$ 192.26	$ 178.41	$ 172.00	$ 168.87
$ 20000.00	$ 301.58	$ 256.35	$ 237.89	$ 229.34	$ 225.15
$ 25000.00	$ 376.97	$ 320.43	$ 297.36	$ 286.67	$ 281.44
$ 30000.00	$ 452.37	$ 384.52	$ 356.83	$ 344.01	$ 337.73
$ 35000.00	$ 527.76	$ 448.61	$ 416.30	$ 401.34	$ 394.02
$ 40000.00	$ 603.16	$ 512.69	$ 475.77	$ 458.68	$ 450.31
$ 45000.00	$ 678.55	$ 576.78	$ 535.24	$ 516.01	$ 506.60
$ 50000.00	$ 753.94	$ 640.87	$ 594.72	$ 573.35	$ 562.89
$ 55000.00	$ 829.34	$ 704.95	$ 654.19	$ 630.68	$ 619.18
$ 60000.00	$ 904.73	$ 769.04	$ 713.66	$ 688.02	$ 675.46
$ 65000.00	$ 980.13	$ 833.13	$ 773.13	$ 745.35	$ 731.75
$ 70000.00	$ 1055.52	$ 897.22	$ 832.60	$ 802.69	$ 788.04
$ 75000.00	$ 1130.92	$ 961.30	$ 892.07	$ 860.02	$ 844.33
$ 80000.00	$ 1206.31	$ 1025.39	$ 951.54	$ 917.36	$ 900.62
$ 85000.00	$ 1281.71	$ 1089.48	$ 1011.02	$ 974.69	$ 956.91
$ 90000.00	$ 1357.10	$ 1153.56	$ 1070.49	$ 1032.03	$ 1013.20
$ 95000.00	$ 1432.49	$ 1217.65	$ 1129.96	$ 1089.36	$ 1069.48
$ 100000.00	$ 1507.89	$ 1281.74	$ 1189.43	$ 1146.70	$ 1125.77
$ 125000.00	$ 1884.86	$ 1602.17	$ 1486.79	$ 1433.37	$ 1407.22
$ 150000.00	$ 2261.83	$ 1922.60	$ 1784.15	$ 1720.05	$ 1688.66

YEARLY INTEREST RATE = 13.50%

	LOAN LIFE IN YEARS				
PRINCIPAL	10	15	20	25	30
	MONTHLY PAYMENTS				
$ 25.00	$ .38	$ .32	$ .30	$ .29	$ .29
$ 50.00	$ .76	$ .65	$ .60	$ .58	$ .57
$ 100.00	$ 1.52	$ 1.30	$ 1.21	$ 1.17	$ 1.15
$ 200.00	$ 3.05	$ 2.60	$ 2.41	$ 2.33	$ 2.29
$ 300.00	$ 4.57	$ 3.89	$ 3.62	$ 3.50	$ 3.44
$ 400.00	$ 6.09	$ 5.19	$ 4.83	$ 4.66	$ 4.58
$ 500.00	$ 7.61	$ 6.49	$ 6.04	$ 5.83	$ 5.73
$ 1000.00	$ 15.23	$ 12.98	$ 12.07	$ 11.66	$ 11.45
$ 2000.00	$ 30.45	$ 25.97	$ 24.15	$ 23.31	$ 22.91
$ 3000.00	$ 45.68	$ 38.95	$ 36.22	$ 34.97	$ 34.36
$ 4000.00	$ 60.91	$ 51.93	$ 48.29	$ 46.63	$ 45.82
$ 5000.00	$ 76.14	$ 64.92	$ 60.37	$ 58.28	$ 57.27
$ 10000.00	$ 152.27	$ 129.83	$ 120.74	$ 116.56	$ 114.54
$ 15000.00	$ 228.41	$ 194.75	$ 181.11	$ 174.85	$ 171.81
$ 20000.00	$ 304.55	$ 259.66	$ 241.47	$ 233.13	$ 229.08
$ 25000.00	$ 380.69	$ 324.58	$ 301.84	$ 291.41	$ 286.35
$ 30000.00	$ 456.82	$ 389.50	$ 362.21	$ 349.69	$ 343.62
$ 35000.00	$ 532.96	$ 454.41	$ 422.58	$ 407.98	$ 400.89
$ 40000.00	$ 609.10	$ 519.33	$ 482.95	$ 466.26	$ 458.16
$ 45000.00	$ 685.23	$ 584.24	$ 543.32	$ 524.54	$ 515.44
$ 50000.00	$ 761.37	$ 649.16	$ 603.69	$ 582.82	$ 572.71
$ 55000.00	$ 837.51	$ 714.07	$ 664.06	$ 641.10	$ 629.98
$ 60000.00	$ 913.65	$ 778.99	$ 724.42	$ 699.39	$ 687.25
$ 65000.00	$ 989.78	$ 843.91	$ 784.79	$ 757.67	$ 744.52
$ 70000.00	$ 1065.92	$ 908.82	$ 845.16	$ 815.95	$ 801.79
$ 75000.00	$ 1142.06	$ 973.74	$ 905.53	$ 874.23	$ 859.06
$ 80000.00	$ 1218.19	$ 1038.65	$ 965.90	$ 932.52	$ 916.33
$ 85000.00	$ 1294.33	$ 1103.57	$ 1026.27	$ 990.80	$ 973.60
$ 90000.00	$ 1370.47	$ 1168.49	$ 1086.64	$ 1049.08	$ 1030.87
$ 95000.00	$ 1446.61	$ 1233.40	$ 1147.01	$ 1107.36	$ 1088.14
$ 100000.00	$ 1522.74	$ 1298.32	$ 1207.37	$ 1165.64	$ 1145.41
$ 125000.00	$ 1903.43	$ 1622.90	$ 1509.22	$ 1457.06	$ 1431.76
$ 150000.00	$ 2284.11	$ 1947.48	$ 1811.06	$ 1748.47	$ 1718.12

YEARLY INTEREST RATE = 13.75%

	LOAN LIFE IN YEARS				
PRINCIPAL	10	15	20	25	30
	MONTHLY PAYMENTS				
$ 25.00	$ .38	$ .33	$ .31	$ .30	$ .29
$ 50.00	$ .77	$ .66	$ .61	$ .59	$ .58
$ 100.00	$ 1.54	$ 1.31	$ 1.23	$ 1.18	$ 1.17
$ 200.00	$ 3.08	$ 2.63	$ 2.45	$ 2.37	$ 2.33
$ 300.00	$ 4.61	$ 3.94	$ 3.68	$ 3.55	$ 3.50
$ 400.00	$ 6.15	$ 5.26	$ 4.90	$ 4.74	$ 4.66
$ 500.00	$ 7.69	$ 6.57	$ 6.13	$ 5.92	$ 5.83
$ 1000.00	$ 15.38	$ 13.15	$ 12.25	$ 11.85	$ 11.65
$ 2000.00	$ 30.75	$ 26.30	$ 24.51	$ 23.69	$ 23.30
$ 3000.00	$ 46.13	$ 39.45	$ 36.76	$ 35.54	$ 34.95
$ 4000.00	$ 61.51	$ 52.60	$ 49.02	$ 47.39	$ 46.60
$ 5000.00	$ 76.88	$ 65.75	$ 61.27	$ 59.23	$ 58.26
$ 10000.00	$ 153.77	$ 131.50	$ 122.54	$ 118.47	$ 116.51
$ 15000.00	$ 230.65	$ 197.25	$ 183.81	$ 177.70	$ 174.77
$ 20000.00	$ 307.53	$ 263.00	$ 245.08	$ 236.93	$ 233.02
$ 25000.00	$ 384.42	$ 328.75	$ 306.35	$ 296.17	$ 291.28
$ 30000.00	$ 461.30	$ 394.50	$ 367.62	$ 355.40	$ 349.53
$ 35000.00	$ 538.18	$ 460.25	$ 428.89	$ 414.63	$ 407.79
$ 40000.00	$ 615.07	$ 525.99	$ 490.16	$ 473.87	$ 466.04
$ 45000.00	$ 691.95	$ 591.74	$ 551.43	$ 533.10	$ 524.30
$ 50000.00	$ 768.83	$ 657.49	$ 612.70	$ 592.33	$ 582.56
$ 55000.00	$ 845.72	$ 723.24	$ 673.97	$ 651.57	$ 640.81
$ 60000.00	$ 922.60	$ 788.99	$ 735.24	$ 710.80	$ 699.07
$ 65000.00	$ 999.48	$ 854.74	$ 796.51	$ 770.03	$ 757.32
$ 70000.00	$ 1076.37	$ 920.49	$ 857.78	$ 829.27	$ 815.58
$ 75000.00	$ 1153.25	$ 986.24	$ 919.05	$ 888.50	$ 873.83
$ 80000.00	$ 1230.13	$ 1051.99	$ 980.32	$ 947.73	$ 932.09
$ 85000.00	$ 1307.02	$ 1117.74	$ 1041.59	$ 1006.97	$ 990.35
$ 90000.00	$ 1383.90	$ 1183.49	$ 1102.86	$ 1066.20	$ 1048.60
$ 95000.00	$ 1460.78	$ 1249.24	$ 1164.13	$ 1125.43	$ 1106.86
$ 100000.00	$ 1537.67	$ 1314.99	$ 1225.40	$ 1184.67	$ 1165.11
$ 125000.00	$ 1922.08	$ 1643.73	$ 1531.76	$ 1480.83	$ 1456.39
$ 150000.00	$ 2306.50	$ 1972.48	$ 1838.11	$ 1777.00	$ 1747.67

YEARLY INTEREST RATE = 14.00%

		LOAN LIFE IN YEARS			
PRINCIPAL	10	15	20	25	30
			MONTHLY PAYMENTS		
$ 25.00	$ .39	$ .33	$ .31	$ .30	$ .30
$ 50.00	$ .78	$ .67	$ .62	$ .60	$ .59
$ 100.00	$ 1.55	$ 1.33	$ 1.24	$ 1.20	$ 1.18
$ 200.00	$ 3.11	$ 2.66	$ 2.49	$ 2.41	$ 2.37
$ 300.00	$ 4.66	$ 4.00	$ 3.73	$ 3.61	$ 3.55
$ 400.00	$ 6.21	$ 5.33	$ 4.97	$ 4.82	$ 4.74
$ 500.00	$ 7.76	$ 6.66	$ 6.22	$ 6.02	$ 5.92
$ 1000.00	$ 15.53	$ 13.32	$ 12.44	$ 12.04	$ 11.85
$ 2000.00	$ 31.05	$ 26.63	$ 24.87	$ 24.08	$ 23.70
$ 3000.00	$ 46.58	$ 39.95	$ 37.31	$ 36.11	$ 35.55
$ 4000.00	$ 62.11	$ 53.27	$ 49.74	$ 48.15	$ 47.39
$ 5000.00	$ 77.63	$ 66.59	$ 62.18	$ 60.19	$ 59.24
$ 10000.00	$ 155.27	$ 133.17	$ 124.35	$ 120.38	$ 118.49
$ 15000.00	$ 232.90	$ 199.76	$ 186.53	$ 180.56	$ 177.73
$ 20000.00	$ 310.53	$ 266.35	$ 248.70	$ 240.75	$ 236.97
$ 25000.00	$ 388.17	$ 332.94	$ 310.88	$ 300.94	$ 296.22
$ 30000.00	$ 465.80	$ 399.52	$ 373.06	$ 361.13	$ 355.46
$ 35000.00	$ 543.43	$ 466.11	$ 435.23	$ 421.32	$ 414.70
$ 40000.00	$ 621.07	$ 532.70	$ 497.41	$ 481.50	$ 473.95
$ 45000.00	$ 698.70	$ 599.28	$ 559.58	$ 541.69	$ 533.19
$ 50000.00	$ 776.33	$ 665.87	$ 621.76	$ 601.88	$ 592.44
$ 55000.00	$ 853.97	$ 732.46	$ 683.94	$ 662.07	$ 651.68
$ 60000.00	$ 931.60	$ 799.04	$ 746.11	$ 722.26	$ 710.92
$ 65000.00	$ 1009.23	$ 865.63	$ 808.29	$ 782.44	$ 770.17
$ 70000.00	$ 1086.86	$ 932.22	$ 870.46	$ 842.63	$ 829.41
$ 75000.00	$ 1164.50	$ 998.81	$ 932.64	$ 902.82	$ 888.65
$ 80000.00	$ 1242.13	$ 1065.39	$ 994.82	$ 963.01	$ 947.90
$ 85000.00	$ 1319.76	$ 1131.98	$ 1056.99	$ 1023.20	$ 1007.14
$ 90000.00	$ 1397.40	$ 1198.57	$ 1119.17	$ 1083.38	$ 1066.38
$ 95000.00	$ 1475.03	$ 1265.15	$ 1181.34	$ 1143.57	$ 1125.63
$ 100000.00	$ 1552.66	$ 1331.74	$ 1243.52	$ 1203.76	$ 1184.87
$ 125000.00	$ 1940.83	$ 1664.68	$ 1554.40	$ 1504.70	$ 1481.09
$ 150000.00	$ 2329.00	$ 1997.61	$ 1865.28	$ 1805.64	$ 1777.31

YEARLY INTEREST RATE = 14.25%

		LOAN LIFE IN YEARS			
PRINCIPAL	10	15	20	25	30
			MONTHLY PAYMENTS		
$ 25.00	$ .39	$ .34	$ .32	$ .31	$ .30
$ 50.00	$ .78	$ .67	$ .63	$ .61	$ .60
$ 100.00	$ 1.57	$ 1.35	$ 1.26	$ 1.22	$ 1.20
$ 200.00	$ 3.14	$ 2.70	$ 2.52	$ 2.45	$ 2.41
$ 300.00	$ 4.70	$ 4.05	$ 3.79	$ 3.67	$ 3.61
$ 400.00	$ 6.27	$ 5.39	$ 5.05	$ 4.89	$ 4.82
$ 500.00	$ 7.84	$ 6.74	$ 6.31	$ 6.11	$ 6.02
$ 1000.00	$ 15.68	$ 13.49	$ 12.62	$ 12.23	$ 12.05
$ 2000.00	$ 31.35	$ 26.97	$ 25.23	$ 24.46	$ 24.09
$ 3000.00	$ 47.03	$ 40.46	$ 37.85	$ 36.69	$ 36.14
$ 4000.00	$ 62.71	$ 53.94	$ 50.47	$ 48.92	$ 48.19
$ 5000.00	$ 78.39	$ 67.43	$ 63.09	$ 61.15	$ 60.23
$ 10000.00	$ 156.77	$ 134.86	$ 126.17	$ 122.29	$ 120.47
$ 15000.00	$ 235.16	$ 202.29	$ 189.26	$ 183.44	$ 180.70
$ 20000.00	$ 313.55	$ 269.72	$ 252.34	$ 244.59	$ 240.94
$ 25000.00	$ 391.93	$ 337.14	$ 315.43	$ 305.73	$ 301.17
$ 30000.00	$ 470.32	$ 404.57	$ 378.52	$ 366.88	$ 361.41
$ 35000.00	$ 548.71	$ 472.00	$ 441.60	$ 428.02	$ 421.64
$ 40000.00	$ 627.09	$ 539.43	$ 504.69	$ 489.17	$ 481.87
$ 45000.00	$ 705.48	$ 606.86	$ 567.77	$ 550.32	$ 542.11
$ 50000.00	$ 783.87	$ 674.29	$ 630.86	$ 611.46	$ 602.34
$ 55000.00	$ 862.25	$ 741.72	$ 693.95	$ 672.61	$ 662.58
$ 60000.00	$ 940.64	$ 809.15	$ 757.03	$ 733.76	$ 722.81
$ 65000.00	$ 1019.02	$ 876.58	$ 820.12	$ 794.90	$ 783.05
$ 70000.00	$ 1097.41	$ 944.01	$ 883.20	$ 856.05	$ 843.28
$ 75000.00	$ 1175.80	$ 1011.43	$ 946.29	$ 917.20	$ 903.51
$ 80000.00	$ 1254.18	$ 1078.86	$ 1009.37	$ 978.34	$ 963.75
$ 85000.00	$ 1332.57	$ 1146.29	$ 1072.46	$ 1039.49	$ 1023.98
$ 90000.00	$ 1410.96	$ 1213.72	$ 1135.55	$ 1100.63	$ 1084.22
$ 95000.00	$ 1489.34	$ 1281.15	$ 1198.63	$ 1161.78	$ 1144.45
$ 100000.00	$ 1567.73	$ 1348.58	$ 1261.72	$ 1222.93	$ 1204.69
$ 125000.00	$ 1959.66	$ 1685.72	$ 1577.15	$ 1528.66	$ 1505.86
$ 150000.00	$ 2351.60	$ 2022.87	$ 1892.58	$ 1834.39	$ 1807.03

YEARLY INTEREST RATE = 14.50%

LOAN LIFE IN YEARS

MONTHLY PAYMENTS

PRINCIPAL	10	15	20	25	30
$ 25.00	$ .40	$ .34	$ .32	$ .31	$ .31
$ 50.00	$ .79	$ .68	$ .64	$ .62	$ .61
$ 100.00	$ 1.58	$ 1.37	$ 1.28	$ 1.24	$ 1.22
$ 200.00	$ 3.17	$ 2.73	$ 2.56	$ 2.48	$ 2.45
$ 300.00	$ 4.75	$ 4.10	$ 3.84	$ 3.73	$ 3.67
$ 400.00	$ 6.33	$ 5.46	$ 5.12	$ 4.97	$ 4.90
$ 500.00	$ 7.91	$ 6.83	$ 6.40	$ 6.21	$ 6.12
$ 1000.00	$ 15.83	$ 13.66	$ 12.80	$ 12.42	$ 12.25
$ 2000.00	$ 31.66	$ 27.31	$ 25.60	$ 24.84	$ 24.49
$ 3000.00	$ 47.49	$ 40.97	$ 38.40	$ 37.26	$ 36.74
$ 4000.00	$ 63.31	$ 54.62	$ 51.20	$ 49.69	$ 48.98
$ 5000.00	$ 79.14	$ 68.28	$ 64.00	$ 62.11	$ 61.23
$ 10000.00	$ 158.29	$ 136.55	$ 128.00	$ 124.22	$ 122.46
$ 15000.00	$ 237.43	$ 204.83	$ 192.00	$ 186.32	$ 183.68
$ 20000.00	$ 316.57	$ 273.10	$ 256.00	$ 248.43	$ 244.91
$ 25000.00	$ 395.72	$ 341.38	$ 320.00	$ 310.54	$ 306.14
$ 30000.00	$ 474.86	$ 409.65	$ 384.00	$ 372.65	$ 367.37
$ 35000.00	$ 554.00	$ 477.93	$ 448.00	$ 434.76	$ 428.59
$ 40000.00	$ 633.15	$ 546.20	$ 512.00	$ 496.86	$ 489.82
$ 45000.00	$ 712.29	$ 614.48	$ 576.00	$ 558.97	$ 551.05
$ 50000.00	$ 791.43	$ 682.75	$ 640.00	$ 621.08	$ 612.28
$ 55000.00	$ 870.58	$ 751.03	$ 704.00	$ 683.19	$ 673.51
$ 60000.00	$ 949.72	$ 819.30	$ 768.00	$ 745.30	$ 734.73
$ 65000.00	$1028.86	$ 887.58	$ 832.00	$ 807.41	$ 795.96
$ 70000.00	$1108.01	$ 955.85	$ 896.00	$ 869.51	$ 857.19
$ 75000.00	$1187.15	$1024.13	$ 960.00	$ 931.62	$ 918.42
$ 80000.00	$1266.29	$1092.40	$1024.00	$ 993.73	$ 979.64
$ 85000.00	$1345.44	$1160.68	$1088.00	$1055.84	$1040.87
$ 90000.00	$1424.58	$1228.95	$1152.00	$1117.95	$1102.10
$ 95000.00	$1503.72	$1297.23	$1216.00	$1180.05	$1163.33
$100000.00	$1582.87	$1365.50	$1280.00	$1242.16	$1224.56
$125000.00	$1978.58	$1706.88	$1600.00	$1552.70	$1530.69
$150000.00	$2374.30	$2048.25	$1920.00	$1863.24	$1836.83

YEARLY INTEREST RATE = 14.75%

LOAN LIFE IN YEARS

MONTHLY PAYMENTS

PRINCIPAL	10	15	20	25	30
$ 25.00	$ .40	$ .35	$ .32	$ .32	$ .31
$ 50.00	$ .80	$ .69	$ .65	$ .63	$ .62
$ 100.00	$ 1.60	$ 1.38	$ 1.30	$ 1.26	$ 1.24
$ 200.00	$ 3.20	$ 2.77	$ 2.60	$ 2.52	$ 2.49
$ 300.00	$ 4.79	$ 4.15	$ 3.90	$ 3.78	$ 3.73
$ 400.00	$ 6.39	$ 5.53	$ 5.19	$ 5.05	$ 4.98
$ 500.00	$ 7.99	$ 6.91	$ 6.49	$ 6.31	$ 6.22
$ 1000.00	$ 15.98	$ 13.83	$ 12.98	$ 12.61	$ 12.44
$ 2000.00	$ 31.96	$ 27.65	$ 25.97	$ 25.23	$ 24.89
$ 3000.00	$ 47.94	$ 41.48	$ 38.95	$ 37.84	$ 37.33
$ 4000.00	$ 63.92	$ 55.30	$ 51.93	$ 50.46	$ 49.78
$ 5000.00	$ 79.90	$ 69.13	$ 64.92	$ 63.07	$ 62.22
$ 10000.00	$ 159.81	$ 138.25	$ 129.84	$ 126.15	$ 124.45
$ 15000.00	$ 239.71	$ 207.38	$ 194.75	$ 189.22	$ 186.67
$ 20000.00	$ 319.61	$ 276.50	$ 259.67	$ 252.29	$ 248.90
$ 25000.00	$ 399.52	$ 345.63	$ 324.59	$ 315.37	$ 311.12
$ 30000.00	$ 479.42	$ 414.75	$ 389.51	$ 378.44	$ 373.34
$ 35000.00	$ 559.33	$ 483.88	$ 454.42	$ 441.51	$ 435.57
$ 40000.00	$ 639.23	$ 553.00	$ 519.34	$ 504.59	$ 497.79
$ 45000.00	$ 719.13	$ 622.13	$ 584.26	$ 567.66	$ 560.01
$ 50000.00	$ 799.04	$ 691.25	$ 649.18	$ 630.73	$ 622.24
$ 55000.00	$ 878.94	$ 760.38	$ 714.10	$ 693.81	$ 684.46
$ 60000.00	$ 958.84	$ 829.50	$ 779.01	$ 756.88	$ 746.69
$ 65000.00	$1038.75	$ 898.63	$ 843.93	$ 819.95	$ 808.91
$ 70000.00	$1118.65	$ 967.75	$ 908.85	$ 883.02	$ 871.13
$ 75000.00	$1198.56	$1036.88	$ 973.77	$ 946.10	$ 933.36
$ 80000.00	$1278.46	$1106.00	$1038.68	$1009.17	$ 995.58
$ 85000.00	$1358.36	$1175.13	$1103.60	$1072.24	$1057.80
$ 90000.00	$1438.27	$1244.25	$1168.52	$1135.32	$1120.03
$ 95000.00	$1518.17	$1313.38	$1233.44	$1198.39	$1182.25
$100000.00	$1598.07	$1382.50	$1298.35	$1261.46	$1244.48
$125000.00	$1997.59	$1728.13	$1622.94	$1576.83	$1555.59
$150000.00	$2397.11	$2073.75	$1947.53	$1892.20	$1866.71

YEARLY INTEREST RATE = 15.00%

			LOAN LIFE IN YEARS		
	10	15	20	25	30
PRINCIPAL			MONTHLY PAYMENTS		
$ 25.00	$ .40	$ .35	$ .33	$ .32	$ .32
$ 50.00	$ .81	$ .70	$ .66	$ .64	$ .63
$ 100.00	$ 1.61	$ 1.40	$ 1.32	$ 1.28	$ 1.26
$ 200.00	$ 3.23	$ 2.80	$ 2.63	$ 2.56	$ 2.53
$ 300.00	$ 4.84	$ 4.20	$ 3.95	$ 3.84	$ 3.79
$ 400.00	$ 6.45	$ 5.60	$ 5.27	$ 5.12	$ 5.06
$ 500.00	$ 8.07	$ 7.00	$ 6.58	$ 6.40	$ 6.32
$ 1000.00	$ 16.13	$ 14.00	$ 13.17	$ 12.81	$ 12.64
$ 2000.00	$ 32.27	$ 27.99	$ 26.34	$ 25.62	$ 25.29
$ 3000.00	$ 48.40	$ 41.99	$ 39.50	$ 38.42	$ 37.93
$ 4000.00	$ 64.53	$ 55.98	$ 52.67	$ 51.23	$ 50.58
$ 5000.00	$ 80.67	$ 69.98	$ 65.84	$ 64.04	$ 63.22
$ 10000.00	$ 161.33	$ 139.96	$ 131.68	$ 128.08	$ 126.44
$ 15000.00	$ 242.00	$ 209.94	$ 197.52	$ 192.12	$ 189.67
$ 20000.00	$ 322.67	$ 279.92	$ 263.36	$ 256.17	$ 252.89
$ 25000.00	$ 403.34	$ 349.90	$ 329.20	$ 320.21	$ 316.11
$ 30000.00	$ 484.00	$ 419.88	$ 395.04	$ 384.25	$ 379.33
$ 35000.00	$ 564.67	$ 489.86	$ 460.88	$ 448.29	$ 442.56
$ 40000.00	$ 645.34	$ 559.83	$ 526.72	$ 512.33	$ 505.78
$ 45000.00	$ 726.01	$ 629.81	$ 592.56	$ 576.37	$ 569.00
$ 50000.00	$ 806.67	$ 699.79	$ 658.39	$ 640.41	$ 632.22
$ 55000.00	$ 887.34	$ 769.77	$ 724.23	$ 704.46	$ 695.44
$ 60000.00	$ 968.01	$ 839.75	$ 790.07	$ 768.50	$ 758.67
$ 65000.00	$1048.68	$ 909.73	$ 855.91	$ 832.54	$ 821.89
$ 70000.00	$1129.34	$ 979.71	$ 921.75	$ 896.58	$ 885.11
$ 75000.00	$1210.01	$1049.69	$ 987.59	$ 960.62	$ 948.33
$ 80000.00	$1290.68	$1119.67	$1053.43	$1024.66	$1011.55
$ 85000.00	$1371.35	$1189.65	$1119.27	$1088.71	$1074.78
$ 90000.00	$1452.01	$1259.63	$1185.11	$1152.75	$1138.00
$ 95000.00	$1532.68	$1329.61	$1250.95	$1216.79	$1201.22
$100000.00	$1613.35	$1399.59	$1316.79	$1280.83	$1264.44
$125000.00	$2016.69	$1749.48	$1645.99	$1601.04	$1580.55
$150000.00	$2420.02	$2099.38	$1975.18	$1921.24	$1896.67

YEARLY INTEREST RATE = 15.25%

			LOAN LIFE IN YEARS		
	10	15	20	25	30
PRINCIPAL			MONTHLY PAYMENTS		
$ 25.00	$ .41	$ .35	$ .33	$ .33	$ .32
$ 50.00	$ .81	$ .71	$ .67	$ .65	$ .64
$ 100.00	$ 1.63	$ 1.42	$ 1.34	$ 1.30	$ 1.28
$ 200.00	$ 3.26	$ 2.83	$ 2.67	$ 2.60	$ 2.57
$ 300.00	$ 4.89	$ 4.25	$ 4.01	$ 3.90	$ 3.85
$ 400.00	$ 6.51	$ 5.67	$ 5.34	$ 5.20	$ 5.14
$ 500.00	$ 8.14	$ 7.08	$ 6.68	$ 6.50	$ 6.42
$ 1000.00	$ 16.29	$ 14.17	$ 13.35	$ 13.00	$ 12.84
$ 2000.00	$ 32.57	$ 28.33	$ 26.71	$ 26.01	$ 25.69
$ 3000.00	$ 48.86	$ 42.50	$ 40.06	$ 39.01	$ 38.53
$ 4000.00	$ 65.15	$ 56.67	$ 53.41	$ 52.01	$ 51.38
$ 5000.00	$ 81.43	$ 70.84	$ 66.76	$ 65.01	$ 64.22
$ 10000.00	$ 162.87	$ 141.67	$ 133.53	$ 130.03	$ 128.45
$ 15000.00	$ 244.30	$ 212.51	$ 200.29	$ 195.04	$ 192.67
$ 20000.00	$ 325.74	$ 283.35	$ 267.06	$ 260.05	$ 256.89
$ 25000.00	$ 407.17	$ 354.19	$ 333.82	$ 325.06	$ 321.11
$ 30000.00	$ 488.61	$ 425.02	$ 400.59	$ 390.08	$ 385.34
$ 35000.00	$ 570.04	$ 495.86	$ 467.35	$ 455.09	$ 449.56
$ 40000.00	$ 651.48	$ 566.70	$ 534.12	$ 520.10	$ 513.78
$ 45000.00	$ 732.91	$ 637.54	$ 600.88	$ 585.12	$ 578.01
$ 50000.00	$ 814.35	$ 708.37	$ 667.65	$ 650.13	$ 642.23
$ 55000.00	$ 895.78	$ 779.21	$ 734.41	$ 715.14	$ 706.45
$ 60000.00	$ 977.22	$ 850.05	$ 801.18	$ 780.15	$ 770.67
$ 65000.00	$1058.65	$ 920.89	$ 867.94	$ 845.17	$ 834.90
$ 70000.00	$1140.09	$ 991.72	$ 934.71	$ 910.18	$ 899.12
$ 75000.00	$1221.52	$1062.56	$1001.47	$ 975.19	$ 963.34
$ 80000.00	$1302.95	$1133.40	$1068.24	$1040.21	$1027.57
$ 85000.00	$1384.39	$1204.24	$1135.00	$1105.22	$1091.79
$ 90000.00	$1465.82	$1275.07	$1201.77	$1170.23	$1156.01
$ 95000.00	$1547.26	$1345.91	$1268.53	$1235.24	$1220.23
$100000.00	$1628.69	$1416.75	$1335.30	$1300.26	$1284.46
$125000.00	$2035.87	$1770.94	$1669.12	$1625.32	$1605.57
$150000.00	$2443.04	$2125.12	$2002.95	$1950.39	$1926.69

YEARLY INTEREST RATE = 15.50%

LOAN LIFE IN YEARS
MONTHLY PAYMENTS

PRINCIPAL	10	15	20	25	30
$ 25.00	$ .41	$ .36	$ .34	$ .33	$ .33
$ 50.00	$ .82	$ .72	$ .68	$ .66	$ .65
$ 100.00	$ 1.64	$ 1.43	$ 1.35	$ 1.32	$ 1.30
$ 200.00	$ 3.29	$ 2.87	$ 2.71	$ 2.64	$ 2.61
$ 300.00	$ 4.93	$ 4.30	$ 4.06	$ 3.96	$ 3.91
$ 400.00	$ 6.58	$ 5.74	$ 5.42	$ 5.28	$ 5.22
$ 500.00	$ 8.22	$ 7.17	$ 6.77	$ 6.60	$ 6.52
$ 1000.00	$ 16.44	$ 14.34	$ 13.54	$ 13.20	$ 13.05
$ 2000.00	$ 32.88	$ 28.68	$ 27.08	$ 26.39	$ 26.09
$ 3000.00	$ 49.32	$ 43.02	$ 40.62	$ 39.59	$ 39.14
$ 4000.00	$ 65.76	$ 57.36	$ 54.16	$ 52.79	$ 52.18
$ 5000.00	$ 82.21	$ 71.70	$ 67.69	$ 65.99	$ 65.23
$ 10000.00	$ 164.41	$ 143.40	$ 135.39	$ 131.97	$ 130.45
$ 15000.00	$ 246.62	$ 215.10	$ 203.08	$ 197.96	$ 195.68
$ 20000.00	$ 328.82	$ 286.80	$ 270.78	$ 263.95	$ 260.90
$ 25000.00	$ 411.03	$ 358.50	$ 338.47	$ 329.94	$ 326.13
$ 30000.00	$ 493.23	$ 430.20	$ 406.16	$ 395.92	$ 391.35
$ 35000.00	$ 575.44	$ 501.90	$ 473.86	$ 461.91	$ 456.58
$ 40000.00	$ 657.64	$ 573.60	$ 541.55	$ 527.90	$ 521.81
$ 45000.00	$ 739.85	$ 645.30	$ 609.25	$ 593.89	$ 587.03
$ 50000.00	$ 822.05	$ 716.99	$ 676.94	$ 659.87	$ 652.26
$ 55000.00	$ 904.26	$ 788.69	$ 744.63	$ 725.86	$ 717.48
$ 60000.00	$ 986.46	$ 860.39	$ 812.33	$ 791.85	$ 782.71
$ 65000.00	$1068.67	$ 932.09	$ 880.02	$ 857.83	$ 847.94
$ 70000.00	$1150.87	$1003.79	$ 947.72	$ 923.82	$ 913.16
$ 75000.00	$1233.08	$1075.49	$1015.41	$ 989.81	$ 978.39
$ 80000.00	$1315.28	$1147.19	$1083.10	$1055.80	$1043.61
$ 85000.00	$1397.49	$1218.89	$1150.80	$1121.78	$1108.84
$ 90000.00	$1479.69	$1290.59	$1218.49	$1187.77	$1174.06
$ 95000.00	$1561.90	$1362.29	$1286.19	$1253.76	$1239.29
$100000.00	$1644.10	$1433.99	$1353.88	$1319.74	$1304.52
$125000.00	$2055.13	$1792.49	$1692.35	$1649.68	$1630.65
$150000.00	$2466.16	$2150.98	$2030.82	$1979.62	$1956.77

YEARLY INTEREST RATE = 15.75%

LOAN LIFE IN YEARS
MONTHLY PAYMENTS

PRINCIPAL	10	15	20	25	30
$ 25.00	$ .41	$ .36	$ .34	$ .33	$ .33
$ 50.00	$ .83	$ .73	$ .69	$ .67	$ .66
$ 100.00	$ 1.66	$ 1.45	$ 1.37	$ 1.34	$ 1.32
$ 200.00	$ 3.32	$ 2.90	$ 2.75	$ 2.68	$ 2.65
$ 300.00	$ 4.98	$ 4.35	$ 4.12	$ 4.02	$ 3.97
$ 400.00	$ 6.64	$ 5.81	$ 5.49	$ 5.36	$ 5.30
$ 500.00	$ 8.30	$ 7.26	$ 6.86	$ 6.70	$ 6.62
$ 1000.00	$ 16.60	$ 14.51	$ 13.73	$ 13.39	$ 13.25
$ 2000.00	$ 33.19	$ 29.03	$ 27.45	$ 26.79	$ 26.49
$ 3000.00	$ 49.79	$ 43.54	$ 41.18	$ 40.18	$ 39.74
$ 4000.00	$ 66.38	$ 58.05	$ 54.90	$ 53.57	$ 52.98
$ 5000.00	$ 82.98	$ 72.57	$ 68.63	$ 66.96	$ 66.23
$ 10000.00	$ 165.96	$ 145.13	$ 137.25	$ 133.93	$ 132.46
$ 15000.00	$ 248.94	$ 217.70	$ 205.88	$ 200.89	$ 198.69
$ 20000.00	$ 331.92	$ 290.26	$ 274.51	$ 267.86	$ 264.92
$ 25000.00	$ 414.90	$ 362.83	$ 343.13	$ 334.82	$ 331.15
$ 30000.00	$ 497.88	$ 435.39	$ 411.76	$ 401.79	$ 397.38
$ 35000.00	$ 580.85	$ 507.96	$ 480.39	$ 468.75	$ 463.62
$ 40000.00	$ 663.83	$ 580.52	$ 549.01	$ 535.72	$ 529.85
$ 45000.00	$ 746.81	$ 653.09	$ 617.64	$ 602.68	$ 596.08
$ 50000.00	$ 829.79	$ 725.65	$ 686.27	$ 669.64	$ 662.31
$ 55000.00	$ 912.77	$ 798.22	$ 754.89	$ 736.61	$ 728.54
$ 60000.00	$ 995.75	$ 870.78	$ 823.52	$ 803.57	$ 794.77
$ 65000.00	$1078.73	$ 943.35	$ 892.15	$ 870.54	$ 861.00
$ 70000.00	$1161.71	$1015.91	$ 960.77	$ 937.50	$ 927.23
$ 75000.00	$1244.69	$1088.48	$1029.40	$1004.47	$ 993.46
$ 80000.00	$1327.67	$1161.05	$1098.03	$1071.43	$1059.69
$ 85000.00	$1410.65	$1233.61	$1166.65	$1138.40	$1125.92
$ 90000.00	$1493.63	$1306.18	$1235.28	$1205.36	$1192.15
$ 95000.00	$1576.61	$1378.74	$1303.91	$1272.32	$1258.39
$100000.00	$1659.58	$1451.31	$1372.53	$1339.29	$1324.62
$125000.00	$2074.48	$1814.13	$1715.67	$1674.11	$1655.77
$150000.00	$2489.38	$2176.96	$2058.80	$2008.93	$1986.92

YEARLY INTEREST RATE = 16.00%

PRINCIPAL	10	15	LOAN LIFE IN YEARS 20 MONTHLY PAYMENTS	25	30
$ 25.00	$ .42	$ .37	$ .35	$ .34	$ .34
$ 50.00	$ .84	$ .73	$ .70	$ .68	$ .67
$ 100.00	$ 1.68	$ 1.47	$ 1.39	$ 1.36	$ 1.34
$ 200.00	$ 3.35	$ 2.94	$ 2.78	$ 2.72	$ 2.69
$ 300.00	$ 5.03	$ 4.41	$ 4.17	$ 4.08	$ 4.03
$ 400.00	$ 6.70	$ 5.87	$ 5.57	$ 5.44	$ 5.38
$ 500.00	$ 8.38	$ 7.34	$ 6.96	$ 6.79	$ 6.72
$ 1000.00	$ 16.75	$ 14.69	$ 13.91	$ 13.59	$ 13.45
$ 2000.00	$ 33.50	$ 29.37	$ 27.83	$ 27.18	$ 26.90
$ 3000.00	$ 50.25	$ 44.06	$ 41.74	$ 40.77	$ 40.34
$ 4000.00	$ 67.01	$ 58.75	$ 55.65	$ 54.36	$ 53.79
$ 5000.00	$ 83.76	$ 73.44	$ 69.56	$ 67.94	$ 67.24
$ 10000.00	$ 167.51	$ 146.87	$ 139.13	$ 135.89	$ 134.48
$ 15000.00	$ 251.27	$ 220.31	$ 208.69	$ 203.83	$ 201.71
$ 20000.00	$ 335.03	$ 293.74	$ 278.25	$ 271.78	$ 268.95
$ 25000.00	$ 418.78	$ 367.18	$ 347.81	$ 339.72	$ 336.19
$ 30000.00	$ 502.54	$ 440.61	$ 417.38	$ 407.67	$ 403.43
$ 35000.00	$ 586.30	$ 514.05	$ 486.94	$ 475.61	$ 470.66
$ 40000.00	$ 670.05	$ 587.48	$ 556.50	$ 543.56	$ 537.90
$ 45000.00	$ 753.81	$ 660.92	$ 626.06	$ 611.50	$ 605.14
$ 50000.00	$ 837.57	$ 734.35	$ 695.63	$ 679.44	$ 672.38
$ 55000.00	$ 921.32	$ 807.79	$ 765.19	$ 747.39	$ 739.62
$ 60000.00	$1005.08	$ 881.22	$ 834.75	$ 815.33	$ 806.85
$ 65000.00	$1088.83	$ 954.66	$ 904.32	$ 883.28	$ 874.09
$ 70000.00	$1172.59	$1028.09	$ 973.88	$ 951.22	$ 941.33
$ 75000.00	$1256.35	$1101.53	$1043.44	$1019.17	$1008.57
$ 80000.00	$1340.10	$1174.96	$1113.00	$1087.11	$1075.80
$ 85000.00	$1423.86	$1248.40	$1182.57	$1155.05	$1143.04
$ 90000.00	$1507.62	$1321.83	$1252.13	$1223.00	$1210.28
$ 95000.00	$1591.37	$1395.27	$1321.69	$1290.94	$1277.52
$100000.00	$1675.13	$1468.70	$1391.26	$1358.89	$1344.76
$125000.00	$2093.91	$1835.88	$1739.07	$1698.61	$1680.95
$150000.00	$2512.70	$2203.05	$2086.88	$2038.33	$2017.13

INDEX